Praise for *Swim Speed Secrets* by Sheila Taormina

"The concept of 'holding' water and generating propulsion is fundamental to swimming performance, and Sheila's book clearly unlocks the secrets of this through words and vivid underwater photos. It is what every top swimmer trains and searches for each day at practice, and it is what allowed me to win Olympic medals as a teenager and into my 40s."
—*Dara Torres, 12-time Olympic medalist*

"Sheila's book *Swim Speed Secrets* is the best swim manual—PERIOD!"
—*Ashley Whitney, Olympic gold medalist*

"Sheila T. is just 5'2", but she swims like she is 6'2". We still use her as a model for our swimmers today on how to swim the strokes."
—*Jack Bauerle, Team USA Olympic swim coach and head coach of the University of Georgia swim team*

"In her book, Sheila Taormina gives a great understanding of the art of high-performance swimming. With her help, you can stop swimming for survival and start swimming like a pro."
—*Laura Bennett, 2010 ITU #1-ranked swimmer, four-time ITU world triathlon championship medalist, Olympian, and two-time U.S. triathlon champion*

"[*Swim Speed Secrets*] is a ripper! [It was] great to get a no-b.s. perspective on swimming from a champion."
—*Chris McCormack, two-time Ironman® world champion*

"Sheila Taormina's ideas on swimming have influenced me and my swim coaching more than anyone else. Her knowledge, experience, and enthusiasm are unmatched. Her book is the best resource out there to help all different types of athletes improve their swim."
—*Siri Lindley, ITU triathlon world champion and coach to triathlon world champions and Olympic medalists*

"Sheila possesses a great depth of knowledge and passion about swimming that she has often shared with me and many other athletes. Her new book will be a very useful tool to anyone who wants to improve their performance in the water."

—Leanda Cave, ITU triathlon world champion and
ITU long-distance triathlon world champion

"Sheila Taormina may be the greatest athlete in the modern Olympic era. She's the only person I know who has made four Olympic teams in three different sports."

—Jim Richardson, head coach of the
University of Michigan women's swim team

SWIM SPEED SECRETS

FOR SWIMMERS AND TRIATHLETES

SWIM SPEED SECRETS

FOR SWIMMERS AND TRIATHLETES

MASTER THE FREESTYLE TECHNIQUE USED BY
THE WORLD'S FASTEST SWIMMERS

SHEILA TAORMINA

BOULDER, COLORADO

3002 Sterling Circle, Suite 100
Boulder, Colorado 80301-2338 USA
(303) 440-0601 • Fax (303) 444-6788 • E-mail velopress@competitorgroup.com

Distributed in the United States and Canada by Ingram Publisher Services

Library of Congress Cataloging-in-Publication Data
Taormina, Sheila.
Swim speed secrets / Sheila Taormina.
     p. cm.
Includes bibliographical references and index.
ISBN 978-1-934030-88-2 (pbk.: alk. paper)
1. Swimming—Training. 2. Speed. I. Title.
GV837.7.T36 2012
797.21—dc23
                              2012005122

For information on purchasing VeloPress books,
please call (800) 811-4210 ext. 2138 or visit www.velopress.com.

This paper meets the requirements of ANSI/NISO Z39.48-1992 (Permanence of Paper).

Text set in Galliard.

13   14   15   /   10   9   8   7   6   5   4   3

To Greg Phill, my swim coach. You lifted the cement blocks off my shoulders before the Olympic Trials the moment you quoted John Lubbock:

When we have done our best, we should wait the result in peace.

Also, thank you for reminding me that a couple billion people never knew when I had a bad race.

CONTENTS

PREFACE

Since the first edition of this book came out in 2010 (then titled *Call the Suit*), I have enjoyed visits with swim teams and triathlon groups around the world, coaching the vital elements of the swim stroke. The excitement of the people I have met confirmed my suspicion that athletes are willing to work hard to be fast. Feedback from those who read the book or attended a swim clinic taught me a great deal about how I could better convey the concepts in this book. The purpose of this revised edition is to add to the text, to elaborate on descriptions, and to issue warnings on when a concept can be taken too far.

As with the previous edition, this revised edition is short for the sake of keeping our focus on the elements of the swim stroke that have the most dramatic impact on performance. The updates are subtle yet important. I have tried to make every sentence count, so be sure to pay close attention.

Thank you for your enthusiasm. I continue to learn from and be inspired by every one of you.

—Sheila T.

ACKNOWLEDGMENTS

First, thank you to my mom and dad.

Mom, for your prayers above all else—but also because, despite being a woman who says she is made of bubble gum and rubber bands, and who has never been seen getting her hair wet at a pool, and who, if I asked her today to tell me what my best 200 freestyle time was, would say something like 3 minutes because she has no clue about times, for all that, you made the perfect swimming mom. Dad, for your ability, after 89 years on this earth, to sum up your life in four words and for the great swim lessons, you are my hero.

To my twin brother, Steven, for copyediting the first round of this book and for keeping Doc Counsilman's swim-camp pamphlet with the revealing underwater photos that I stared at for hours before 1996. Growing up with you as my number-one friend and playmate is a treasure worth more than all the gold in the world.

To every sister and brother, niece and nephew, and brother- and sister-in-law, thank you for coming to all four Olympics and cheering just as wildly for a 23rd-place finish as for a gold-medal finish. You know about the true spirit of human endeavor. You are what I love most about life.

To my swim coach Greg Phill, to whom this book is dedicated. If you were taken out of the time line of my life, the sports story would begin and end completely differently. And to your amazing wife, Jules—my friend in "the Truth."

To my college coaches, Jack Bauerle and Harvey Humphries at the University of Georgia. There will never be a more perfect duo. I've watched with admiration as you have built the Georgia program to number one in the country, and I know the foundation upon which it lies is authentic, balanced, and as much about life as it is about swimming. I am so thankful for all of your guidance and love.

To Jack Nelson, Fort Lauderdale Swim Team. Coach, you have the most beautiful, believing mind. I am thankful that even a sliver of that belief seeped into my own mind, because technique alone does not win a race. You will go down in history as a coach who took the impossible and made it possible because of belief—the 1976 women's 4 × 100 freestyle relay team that brought home gold against East Germany. You are a rock star, and so is every girl on that team!

To Jim Richardson, head women's swim coach at the University of Michigan, thank you for making available, on a daily basis, the university's 50-m pool before 1996. The encouragement you gave Greg and me during those days was a true gift, and your dry-erase-board lessons on swimming technique opened new levels of understanding for me.

To Greyson and Georgie Quarles for your genuine friendship, and for welcoming my cats and me to your house in the warm Florida Keys during the winter of 2010 so that I could write this book. Thank you for sharing your blessings. (P.S. The cats want to go back . . . no pressure—I'm just relaying the message.)

To Matt Farrell at United States Swimming for tracking down historical information and Olympic swimming footage for my personal research. The timeliness with which you responded to my request was exceptional and so very much appreciated.

To Craig Askins from Lane Gainer, not only for supporting my swimming, triathlon, and modern pentathlon careers but also for your help on the technical aspects of taking underwater photos for this book.

To Dave Tanner and Joel Stager, who are carrying the torch forward to preserve, and build upon, the work of Doc Counsilman, the greatest pioneer in the history of swimming. You two, in that cubbyhole office on Indiana University's campus, have a hidden jewel. It was an honor to meet you and see Doc's original cameras and equipment. Also, thank you for granting permission to reprint Doc's original photos of Mike Troy and Mark Spitz.

To Stan Gerbig, photographer at Indiana University, for giving an entire day to take early test rounds of underwater photos. Your generosity helped get this book off the ground.

To my brother-in-law David for taking the very first underwater test pictures at Eastern Michigan University with last-minute notice . . . so very much appreciated! And to Peter Linn, head swim coach at Eastern Michigan University, for arranging the pool availability for those photos.

To Jeff Kempf, pool supervisor at Whitmore Lake High School, for opening the pool and giving countless hours of your time while the final photos for the book were captured. And to Denise Kerrigan, Whitmore Lake Community Recreation and Athletics director, for supporting the project by granting permission to use the pool. Thank you so much.

To Rolf Zettersten for your professional opinion and guidance into the world of publishing and writing. Your encouragement gave me the confidence to see this project through.

To Bruce Wigo, executive director at the International Swimming Hall of Fame in Fort Lauderdale, for your wonderful support in tracking down historical information and for granting permission to use Johnny Weissmuller's photo. Thank you for all you do to preserve swimming history.

To Daniel Smith for the exceptional final photos you captured for this book. Simply put, you are a champion of life. Thank you for making time in your busy schedule, driving back and forth to Michigan, to work on this project. Your creativity and work ethic are far beyond what I could have hoped or asked for from you.

To Jim Cahill for your graciousness in being the subject of "the low elbow." When the guys give you grief for that, just show them your marathon time. Mostly, thank you for your wonderful friendship.

A special thanks to Price Fishback, my economics professor at the University of Georgia. Price, thank you for making a potentially dry subject incredibly applicable to life. Also, to my production management and business professors at the University of Georgia—Jim Cox, Gerald Horton, and James Gilbert—for your gifted teaching and genuine interest in my swimming career.

To Elizabeth Haverkate for brewing up countless lattes, mochas, and espressos. They were fantastic!

To Peter Vanderkaay, Allison Schmitt, and Margaret Kelley for taking time from your busy schedules to come to the pool for the photos. You represent the sport of swimming beautifully. I wish you all great success as you carry the torch in 2012 and beyond. And to Allison's parents, Ralph and Gail Schmitt—thank you for giving up your daughter for a half day during her short visit home.

To Eric Baumgartner, assistant athletic director at the University of Georgia, for providing the National Collegiate Athletic Association compliance information in such a timely manner.

And finally, to the crew at VeloPress in Boulder—notably Dave Trendler, Ted Costantino, Renee Jardine, Kara Mannix, Sonia Smith, and Casey Blaine—from our first meeting in 2011 and throughout the yearlong process, each of you has patiently and professionally guided the project. Thank you for the opportunity to take this book to levels I would have never been able to do. A special thank you is extended to Casey Blaine for your intuitiveness in editing the book without compromising my voice or the book's essence. You have my deepest respect and admiration for your talents, and my sincere thanks for making the work enjoyable.

Above all, a thank you to God for blessing my life with health, opportunity, the people mentioned in this book, and many others beyond.

INTRODUCTION

How is it that the elite swimmers in the 2008 Olympics in Beijing and 2009 World Championships in Rome dizzyingly tore apart almost every world record, while masses of triathletes, masters swimmers, and age groupers remain stumped as to why their times are barely improving, or not improving at all?

The elite swimming times are almost unreal. Consider for a moment that the women's world records are now as fast as the men's world records from the early 1970s. That means that even Mark Spitz's times from the 1972 Olympic Games are being met by the fastest women today. The 200-m freestyle is a perfect example. Today's world record for women is 1:52.98, while Spitz won Olympic gold in Munich in 1:52.78.

It doesn't matter which stroke you choose, or which distance. In the 50-m freestyle, South African Jonty Skinner held the world record in 1976 with a time of 23.86. On August 2, 2009, Britta Steffen of Germany powered to a 23.73. Today's 1500-m freestyle world record for women, 15:42.54, is 10 seconds faster than the gold medal, world record–setting time for men at the 1972 Olympics.

The elite male swimmers are doing the same thing the women are doing—smashing previous marks at a rate that has left most people scratching their heads. It makes a statement made by the famous Johnny Weissmuller seem almost comical. Weissmuller, who won five Olympic gold medals in swimming at the 1924 and 1928 games, stated in his book *Swimming the American Crawl*, in the chapter "Can the Crawl Be Improved?":

My technique has been called the "perfected" crawl stroke because it reduced water resistance to the minimum; it facilitated a method of breathing that most closely approximates the natural, involuntary method of nature; it put the body in a position to make free and unimpeded use of all its strength and power and leverage, and it got the most propulsion for the effort expended. Some say there is still room for improvement in this stroke. I do not see just where the improvement will come. (Weissmuller 1930, 45)

Now, we have to give Weissmuller some slack for thinking the world would never improve upon what he did in the roaring '20s, because he did set 67 world records during his swimming career. In fact, he was never beaten in an official swimming race. Think about it—*never* beaten! If I were him, I probably would have thought I had perfected the crawl too. Also, it wasn't like he just dove in and swam any old way he wanted. In his book, he describes—down to the smallest detail—the reasons why he used the technique he used. A great deal of thought went into it.

What was that technique? You may know it as the Tarzan drill—the drill you do in practice where you hold your head above the water. If your coach is a fun person, then he or she will insist you do the ululating Tarzan yell while you stroke (mine did).

That was Weissmuller's stroke, keeping his chest and shoulders high in the water, and the drill is called the Tarzan drill because Weissmuller became even more famous after his swimming career when he landed the role of Tarzan in the movies. Below is another excerpt from his book in which he describes his stroke:

I swim with my chest and shoulders high in the water. This enables me to hydroplane, like a speedboat, reducing resistance to a minimum. I swim higher in the water than anybody ever did before, higher than anybody else does to this day. . . . The height of my chest enables me to arch my back, avoiding the strain of the swayback position which many have to take in order to get the face out of the water for inhaling. The high chest and shoulders and the arch of the back throw my feet lower in the water, where they maintain traction at all times. (Weissmuller 1930, 20)

JOHNNY WEISSMULLER (AKA TARZAN), SWIMMING WITH THE STROKE THAT EARNED HIM 5 OLYMPIC GOLD MEDALS AND 67 WORLD RECORDS

Continuing on, Weissmuller wrote that he also believed the hips should stay flat, because, as he explains, if the hips roll, then the corresponding arm and shoulder dip lower in the water, thus causing resistance.

Today's freestyle swim technique we know to be the exact opposite. The only people holding their heads above water are people who do not want to get their hair wet, like my mom, and using the hips as part of the stroke is most certainly on everyone's radar.

So, are you wondering where I'm going with this?

If you think we are headed for a discussion on reducing resistance, then guess again. Rather, I am going to use Weissmuller and a number of other swimmers who have reigned as champions in the pool for the past five decades to present a picture of swimming that is long overdue—a picture that answers a great many questions.

To begin painting this picture, let me set the scene with the following shocking information: Even though Weissmuller's times have long been shattered (his 100-m freestyle world record was first broken in 1934), his fastest 100-m freestyle still beats

95 percent of triathletes (even the top professionals), 95 percent of masters swimmers, and 95 percent of age-group swimmers today. It is indeed strange commentary that Weissmuller would beat just about every person reading this book.

Let's look at his times: In February 1924, Weissmuller swam a 57.4 in the 100-m freestyle (long course meters). Sure, the world record now is 46.91, set by Cesar Cielo of Brazil (2009 World Championships), and the women's world record is 52.07 (Britta Steffen, Germany, 2009 World Championships), but how many of you who are reading this book would think you were the cat's meow for going a time like Weissmuller's?

And it wasn't just the short races in which Weissmuller set world records. He also owned the 400-m and 800-m freestyle records: 4:57.0 in the 400, set in 1923, and 10:22.2 in the 800, set in 1927. Although not nearly as impressive as his 100-m freestyle time, those distance event times would still, even today, place him in the lead, or very near the lead, at any triathlon event going into T-1 (Transition 1, which is triathlon talk for the changeover from the swim to the bike).

I realize that Weissmuller's times may not impress all of you in the swimming world today, especially his 400 and 800 times (Weissmuller was definitely more of a sprinter than a distance swimmer), which means at this point some of you may think this book is too elementary. It may appear that I am going to address only the crowd that needs to catch up with swimming times that were posted almost 100 years ago. Don't close the book so fast. This book is invaluable for a swimmer with national times, or the coach of a swimmer with those times, because it is as much about thought processes as it is about swim technique. You may be on the verge of cracking into the very top of the elite ranks but wonder how you are going to climb the next rung of the ladder. The insights provided in this book will help you do that.

The reason many of us have been stumped about how to make improvements in our times, or how to reach the next level, is not for lack of information but rather for lack of organization of the information. Some swimmers try to work on everything, which means they are working on nothing at all. Other swimmers are working on things that have minimal to zero impact on their times, because they were never accurately told what is most important and which things must be developed first. This book will change that.

You should know why you do what you do at every moment when you are working on technique or training. This is completely possible, yet it is the one thing I see missing in the resources available to date. Textbooks on the market provide us with massive amounts of information—down to the minutest details of stroke technique—but no one has organized the information in a fashion that guides us toward a focus, and thus an effective plan.

I have a mantra, in sport and in life, that is about taking charge. It is "call the suit." In my favorite card game, Euchre, each player is given the opportunity at various times during the game to call the suit that will be "trump" (most powerful). Players must look at the hands they were dealt and on their turn make a decision about whether to take charge of the play of the game or pass the opportunity to the next player, their competitor. I always encourage people to "call the suit!" Be bold. Understand what you have in your hand, and then make an informed decision on how best to play the game from there.

We are seldom coached on how to do this in our lives. My goal is to show the thought process that will develop this in your swimming, and it will actually be a launching pad for you to apply it to other areas of your life as well.

I've limited the book to the discussion of one stroke—freestyle—for two reasons. First, I wanted to write a book for triathletes more than any other group. I feel that this group has latched on to one swim-technique theory for too long. They have been given only small parts of what they need to know about swimming and led to believe it is what "swimmers" do. I want to show triathletes the real picture of what swimmers do.

The second reason for focusing only on freestyle is simply because it is the stroke that I know inside and out. It is the stroke that took me to the Olympics four times. I studied it, I spent endless moments thinking about it in the pool, and I got to know it. I am a fraction of an inch over 5 foot 2 inches in height, so my wingspan was not what put me on the Olympic team—it was the understanding of how to take information and make it work.

If you are new to swimming, please do not be intimidated by this book. The principles are simple. You will understand everything, and it will help you see the path to your goals.

Last, and perhaps most important, let's keep everything in perspective—we are not solving any world crisis here. Let's have fun. I am almost certain that if I had had to give up coffee in order to do sports, then I probably would have given up sports. (OK, I'm joking . . . maybe.) Make sure to read the dedication if you need additional perspective, and let's move forward with answering the question from the beginning of this introduction.

Here's wishing you joy on your journey to understanding the beautiful sport of swimming.

USA OLYMPIC TEAM MEMBERS
ALLISON SCHMITT AND
SHEILA TAORMINA SHOWING
THAT FAST SWIMMING ISN'T
JUST ABOUT WING SPAN!

THE PARETO PRINCIPLE
APPLYING THE 80/20 RULE IN THE POOL

Swimming is an incredibly dynamic sport. Every part of your body is doing something all of the time when you swim competitively. Even the head, which stays neutral and steady, needs to be turned for the breath. It can be an information-management nightmare, not only for beginners trying to learn the sport but also for experienced swimmers who are at a loss to identify exactly what they are missing that will take them to the next level.

In case you have never thought about the complexity of the task, let's contrast swimming with other sports that are less dynamic in terms of technique. The examples that follow are two disciplines with which I am very familiar, having experienced both on the Olympic stage.

Pistol shooting. There are great challenges in this sport (remaining focused and calm under pressure, for example), but the technique is very static. A pistol shooter methodically progresses through each step in the process, focusing on one element of the sequence at a time, until the shot is fired. Therefore, the training of shooting technique is not overwhelming. Remaining composed under competition pressure? That is a completely different story, for another book.

Cycling. This sport falls in the middle of the static-dynamic spectrum. While the legs are dynamically powering the pedal stroke, the upper body is quite still. Anytime a cyclist chooses to focus on technique, a smoother pedal stroke, for example, she needs only to focus on the lower half of the body. Therefore, the learning curve and application of technique are quite manageable. The keys to success for this sport are as difficult as in any other sport, but mentally managing technique is not one of them.

Managing technique in swimming, compared with these other sports, is a beast of a task. During any given length of the pool, a swimmer may choose to perfect one of many elements of the stroke. While working on that one element, the swimmer must also consider how to make it work synchronously with the other parts of the stroke. Then throw in the fact that this is managed within a medium that is not natural to humans—water—and the recipe can be overwhelming. My guess is that, because of all this, a high percentage of the people who are reading this book are frustrated as to why their swimming times have not improved after all the hours they have spent in the pool. I hear you. I went through the same frustrations with fencing when learning that for the pentathlon.

Fencing, like swimming, is incredibly dynamic. Every body part is doing something all the time, even down to the fingers that hold the grip, and the timing of every body part is crucial. Although the sport is contested in a natural environment for the athlete—land—its true complexity is revealed when the athlete is faced with another human being on the other side of the competition strip thwarting every attempted move. During the years I tried to grasp each detail of fencing technique, from age 36 to 39, my coaches continually yelled, in thick Eastern European accents, "Why you do that?" If I was thinking about my arm, then my legs were messing up; if I was thinking about my footwork, then I missed the timing. One coach would tell me to lean forward more, and another coach would say to stand up more. There was so much to think about simultaneously that I didn't know where to start, nor did I know which coach to trust.

Believe me, I empathize with anyone learning the sport of swimming and with those who have been at it for a while but have seen no improvements in performance. I also relate to the huge population of coaches and swimmers who have experienced a fair amount of success in swimming but who want to know what it takes to reach the next level, or perhaps to crack the elite ranks one day.

The good news is, while I cannot help you with your fencing, I can definitely help with your swimming. What we have to do is begin sorting and organizing the information.

VILREDO PARETO, ITALIAN INDUSTRIALIST, ECONOMIST, AND PHILOSOPHER

EMPLOYING THE PARETO PRINCIPLE

Because swimming is so dynamic, the only way to get a solid grip on where to start is to manage all the information. The best way I know of sorting information is to employ the Pareto principle, also known as the 80/20 rule. The Pareto principle is not a hard-and-fast rule; rather, it is applied as a rule of thumb, most commonly in arenas such as business and science. When I first learned about it in 1993, I saw immediately how it could be a tool for sports. I applied it to my swimming before the 1996 Olympics and to every sport I have done since.

Vilfredo Pareto was an Italian economist who, in the early 1900s, took note that approximately 80 percent of the wealth in his country belonged to 20 percent of the people. After his notation, others realized that you could apply this 80/20 concept to many aspects of life. In business, a salesperson might note that 80 percent of sales come from 20 percent of clients, or that 80 percent of problems come from 20 percent of clients. In our personal lives, we may note that we spend 80 percent of our time with 20 percent of our acquaintances, and so on.

The Pareto principle is also known as the law of the vital few. It says that there are a few aspects (20 percent) of anything we do that have the greatest impact (80 percent) on what we are trying to accomplish. The other 80 percent of things, added together, do not have nearly the same impact as those vital few.

In a sport, if we can identify the vital few things that give the greatest impact, then we are much better equipped to design an effective plan that brings us closer to our goal. We do not ignore the other 80 percent of things that give us some return; we simply know where they fall in the list of priorities.

In this book, I am going to show you the vital few items of swimming technique. They are extremely important. They give us 80 percent of what we need to be a fast swimmer. Every other detail in our technique does not influence our swimming results nearly as much as the vital few. Another way to look at it is that the other details give us minimal benefit unless we have mastered the vital few.

Although I will still address a few other aspects of swim technique, this book is focused more on helping you develop the big whoppers. Believe it or not, most people are not working on those. Instead, I see them working on the 80 percent of things that give little return or that give no return without the foundation of the vital few.

There is no top-secret training manual that gold medalists have. The best swimmers in the world do the vital few elements really well, and they think about them most of the time. I even dare to say they think about them 80 percent of the time during practice—warm-up included.

TECHNIQUE IS 80 PERCENT OF SWIMMING

When you are swimming up and down the pool, you are usually alone with your own thoughts, right? That is when I hope you are working on your swim technique instead of being off in la-la land. Coaches stand over your lane every once in a while, but for the most part you are in charge of whether you are thinking about technique or what's for dinner.

I have to drive home the point that technique is, by far, the most important aspect of swimming. There is no reason why we cannot apply the 80/20 rule here, and I am going to make the bold claim that technique is 80 percent of swimming when lined up next to strength, conditioning, or the size of a swimmer.

Conditioning and strength are very important in swimming, but they will not get you far without good technique. Ask the strongest football player you know to swim one length of the pool. If he has not learned technique, then he will look like a drowning rat in the water, and it is not because his muscles are weighing him down. It is the same with conditioning. You could ask a sub-2:40 marathoner to swim, and if she does not know swim technique, then all the conditioning in the world will not help. This is one of the scenarios in which the vital elements are important because they are the foundation upon which the other elements rely. Technique takes the 80 percent prize because without it strength and conditioning mean nothing. That being said, once we have developed a solid technique, then the ratios change, and our physical training kicks in much more.

I see too many athletes allowing their strokes to fall apart when they tire at practice. Or, worse, I see people choosing to forgo technique altogether and thrash at the water in order to keep up with their lane mates. The only way you will benefit from reading this book is if you commit to making the vital elements of swim technique a priority.

In fact, my goal is to get you so excited about your understanding of swimming technique after reading this book that you actually become addicted to making that your focus during practice. Then, once you're on a good roll with technique, the training, conditioning, and strength become fascinating and much more meaningful.

You are probably getting antsy by now to find out which are the vital few elements and may want to skip ahead to find them. Don't do that just yet. We have to go over the big-picture understanding of swimming first. After that, we will begin to name the vital few and explain how to develop them. Remember the 80/20 rule, though, because I will refer to it later.

So, in honor of Vilfredo, brew up a good Italian-roast espresso, take a comfortable seat, and enjoy the next few chapters.

1. **The Pareto principle,** also known as the 80/20 rule, is the law of the vital few. We will get our greatest impact (approximately 80 percent) from only a few (approximately 20 percent) of the things we do.

2. In swimming, **technique** is the one aspect that takes us 80 percent of the way to being a great swimmer. Conditioning and strength do not help us as swimmers if we first do not have good technique.

3. At **swim practice**, swimmers should maintain focus on technique instead of getting sloppy when they are tired or forgoing technique altogether in order to keep up with the other people in their lane.

2

THE BIG PICTURE

UNDERSTANDING THE SWIMMING EQUATION

Are you ready? You may be surprised to see how straightforward the concepts in this book are. In this chapter, you will be presented with the big-picture view of swimming, perhaps for the first time. Once you understand the big picture, the details of technique will begin to make much more sense. You will be able to answer many of the questions about technique for yourself, and your swimming will go to a whole new level. You will have confidence, and the laps up and down the pool will begin to mean something. The best part is how simple it all is.

First, let's set the stage (see Figure 2.1): You are going to push off the wall and swim 25 yards. We will assume that you begin the 25-yard swim with a good

FIGURE 2.1

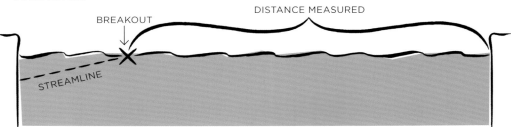

underwater streamline—a contoured body position used by swimmers to reduce water resistance after diving into a pool or pushing off a wall. The vast majority of elite competitive swimmers employ an underwater streamline for 2–5 seconds before surfacing to begin stroking.

Now you are on the surface swimming.

Only two things affect the time it takes you to get from your breakout (the moment a swimmer surfaces and begins stroking after streamlining underwater) to the end of the pool. These two factors are not the "vital few" elements from our Pareto principle discussion; we will get to those soon. However, these two key factors make up the swimming equation that frames the big picture:

1. The number of strokes you take to get across the pool
2. The rate at which you take those strokes (turnover)

NUMBER OF STROKES AND RATE

Let's say that it takes you 10 strokes (full arm cycles) to get to the end of the pool. Let's also say it takes you 1 second per stroke.

If you multiply the number of strokes by the rate at which you take those strokes, then you get your time. Here is what it looks like in equation form:

$$\textbf{(Number of Strokes)} \times \textbf{(Rate of Turnover)} = \textbf{Time (in seconds)}$$

Remember: One stroke is a full arm cycle. In other words, one stroke is from the point when one arm enters the water until that same arm enters the water again. A different way to count strokes is to count "one" when the right arm goes in and then "two" when the left arm goes in, and so on. Both methods of counting are equally acceptable, but I have chosen to count full cycles.

Let's insert the numbers from our example:

$$\text{(10 strokes)} \times \text{(1 second/stroke)} = \text{10 seconds}$$

Number of Strokes	Rate of Turnover	Time

Mathematically it looks like this (remember from math class, we cross out the "strokes" in our equation):

$$10 \; \cancel{\text{strokes}} \times \frac{1 \text{ second}}{\cancel{\text{stroke}}} = 10 \text{ seconds}$$

That's it. There is the big picture. You can only get faster in swimming in one of two ways:

1. Reduce the number of strokes you take.
2. Turn over the strokes more quickly.

You just learned what I learned at age 25. I had competed in two Olympic Trials (1988 and 1992) before I learned this simple equation. A new level of understanding opened up for me, and I truly believe this knowledge helped me make my first Olympic team in 1996. You might be tempted to take just this one thing and run with it, but while it is true that only two factors affect our swimming time, many things affect those two factors. Still, we are on our way. We now have the big picture around which we can frame the details of technique. So remember, when you read something about swim technique, or if your coach tells you to change your stroke, ask yourself how it will influence either the number of strokes you take or the rate at which you take them.

THE SWIMMING EQUATION IN PRACTICE

Let's look at the equation more closely and take note of how the two factors work in a real-life situation.

To reduce our time in swimming, the two factors must be lowered. We can either lower one or the other, or both. The tricky part is that sometimes we get excited that we reduced one, but we forget to check how the other was affected.

The two factors are not always independent of each other. Sometimes the steps we take to reduce one factor end up increasing the other. The best way to explain this is to give two examples. (Note: The numbers I am using in these examples are chosen for the sake of simplicity. Chapter 7 examines the actual stroke counts and rate numbers we see in the top swimmers.)

Example 1: Reducing Strokes

A weekend swimming clinic is coming to town. It is marketed as holding the key to unleashing your swimming potential. At the clinic, swimmers are told that taking fewer strokes is better. The focus is entirely on reducing the number of strokes to get across the pool. From our equation, we know this is a good thing. However, at this clinic, the swimmers are not told about the other half of the equation.

All weekend, the participants are in the water—reaching, extending, and gliding out front. They look beautiful and smooth.

The athletes get excited about having reduced their number of strokes from 10 down to 8. They probably raised their hands to tell the coach the good news, and the coach probably high-fived them. But, here is the problem: the coach never told them about rate. No one timed their turnover. Now, instead of taking 1 second per stroke, the swimmers are taking 1.5 seconds per stroke, because they are gliding out front so long on every stroke.

By the end of the clinic, their equation looks like this:

$$8 \text{ str\cancel{okes}} \times \frac{1.5 \text{ seconds}}{\text{str\cancel{oke}}} = 12 \text{ seconds}$$

Yikes! They became slower. They left the clinic thinking they had become faster, but the opposite was true. And the reason they got slower was that they were taught only half the equation and led to believe they could improve their swimming by focusing only on reducing their number of strokes.

They may not realize this for a while. In fact, many of them may never quite understand, instead always wondering what they did wrong. I hope this book gets into the hands of everyone who has experienced that disappointment, because I want to tell them that they did nothing wrong. The problem was that they were never given the full picture. They were only given half the equation and thought that was all they needed to be on their way to swimming stardom.

The bottom line is that you cannot improve the *number of strokes* side of the equation by gliding out front. That is not what competitive swimmers do to improve their swim times.

That said, gliding does serve one particular group of swimmers quite well. It serves the swimmer who would like to enjoy the sport simply for exercise or is learning to swim simply to survive through a triathlon or, as a friend of mine once put it, in case your boat sinks. In other words, anyone who is not focused on time and who simply wants the enjoyment of being able to swim (or is a survivalist) will benefit wonderfully from stretching out his or her stroke. It is less taxing, is simple to do, and provides a healthy, low-impact way to exercise.

However, if you are a swimmer who wants to be competitive, then you have to hang with me for a while longer to find out how to reduce the number of strokes you take without adversely affecting your rate.

Example 2: Reducing Rate

For this example, let's imagine a completely different scenario. You are at an age-group swim meet, and the adorable 8 and unders are on the blocks for the 25-yard freestyle. Their goggles are on crooked, their suits are too big for them, and they are ready to jump in and give it their all. They have so much energy stored up that they are like wind-up toys, which is exactly what they look like when they race down the pool. Their arms spin at warp speed. They take about a million strokes to get to the other end. It is the cutest thing ever!

Here is what their equation looks like:

$$15 \text{ s}\cancel{\text{troke}}\text{s} \times \frac{0.8 \text{ seconds}}{\text{s}\cancel{\text{troke}}} = 12 \text{ seconds}$$

The great effort that was just put forth ends up not paying off. The time is slower. Even though the rate side of the equation was reduced, the number of strokes went up significantly, because the arms never "held" the water. This scenario can be likened to a car's wheels spinning on ice.

Most people reading this book will fall into the category of Example 1, but understanding what is going on in Example 2 is important. Learning to "hold" the water is critical. If you are paying close attention to words, then *critical* is your clue that we are getting closer to discussing the 20 percent of stroke elements that take us 80 percent of the way to optimizing both factors in our equation.

1. There are only **two ways to get faster in swimming**:

    a. Take fewer strokes.

    b. Turn over strokes more quickly.

2. The equation to remember:

    (Number of Strokes) × (Rate of Turnover) = Time

3. We must **reduce one or both of the factors** in order to improve our time.

4. Pay attention to both factors **(number of strokes and rate of turnover)** when making a stroke change, because they are not always independent of each other. By lowering one factor you may end up increasing the other factor to the point where the total time is adversely affected.

THE
VITAL ELEMENT

A CASE TO PROVE IT

Now that you understand the swimming equation and the fact that both the number of strokes and the rate of turnover are important, we are ready to move on to what I consider the most vital element in swimming and my argument to prove that claim. But before we dive in, I need first to introduce the topic of water and how to work with it.

Water is a fascinating medium, midway between air and a solid object. Picture yourself trying to grab air. You cannot hold it. You cannot pull yourself forward. (Remember how you tried to fly off your back porch as a kid and went nowhere?) Now, picture yourself holding onto a solid object that is anchored in the ground, like a signpost. If you hold the post with your hand, you can pull your body forward. Your hand stays locked on the post, and your body moves in the direction you pulled. Your hand stays; your body moves.

In essence, water has more substance (viscosity or thickness) than air but is not nearly as solid as an object that is anchored. The especially interesting part about water is that, depending on what we do in it with our body, it can be manipulated in different ways. We can apply pressure to it so that it feels somewhat solid, or we can slip through it like a seal.

As swimmers, we want to work with the water in both of those ways simultaneously. First, consider that swimming is a three-dimensional sport. We have a depth component in addition to the lateral and forward/backward components. It is this depth component that makes swimming different from other sports. Two beautiful dynamics are going on at the same time. One dynamic is taking place on the surface of the water, and the other is taking place deeper in the water, where the arm is pulling.

MAKING WATER SOLID

Let's look first at what takes place deep in the water, where the arm is pulling. Here we want to work with the water to make it as solid as possible.

If you have ever heard someone say, "Wow, she has a great feel for the water" or "Look at the hold he has on the water," then what you were hearing was that the swimmer was doing a great job of making the water below as solid as possible. From the pool deck it may look like the swimmer is moving effortlessly, but in reality there is a lot of work going on beneath the surface. The hand and arm are anchored on the water below, pulling the body over top. Ideally, a swimmer wants to move the body forward, not the hand backward. (See Figure 3.1.)

For all of the out-of-date elements Johnny Weissmuller wrote about in *Swimming the American Crawl,* such as keeping the chest and shoulders high and not using his hips, he was way ahead of his time when it came to the concept of making the water beneath him solid. This 1920s Olympian wrote the following beautiful description: "Water is elusive, but you can get 'hold' of it if you know how to go after it" (Weissmuller 1930, 62).

Another phrase he used to convey the job of holding water was "purchase power." He described how his arm would "feel for the purchase" of the water. Today we use the term *catch.* The catch is essentially the very first moment that we get our hold, or feel, for the water. It happens out front. When our hand enters the water, we grab it, "catch it," "purchase it," and then stay on it—hold it. This is the part of swimming that is most like art rather than science.

There are a number of ways to describe the concepts of "catching" and "holding" the water. A coach once told me to envision a brick wall underneath me.

A THREE-DIMENSIONAL SPORT,
WITH SURFACE COMPONENTS
AND DEPTH COMPONENTS

He said, "Grab a hold of it, lock on, and pull your body over the wall." That vision worked for me. Some coaches, however, believe this is a misrepresentation of what is going on under the water. Cecil Colwin, legendary Australian swimming coach and author of a number of insightful books on technique and training, described it this way in *Breakthrough Swimming*: "To convey the concept of a force acting on a mass of water, the act of propulsion has been variously described as feeling for undisturbed water, anchoring the hand on a fixed spot in the water and pulling the body past it. . . . These descriptions, strictly speaking, are inappropriate because the propulsive force is not applied against a solid or rigid resistance. Coaches should use carefully chosen words when instructing a swimmer" (Colwin 2002, 109).

Colwin is correct; words should be chosen carefully. Water indeed is not a rigid substance. Semantics are important, but keep in mind that a particular description may register for one person while another description turns on the light for someone else. I benefited tremendously from picturing a wall beneath me. We have more to discuss about this concept of the "feel" and "hold" of the "elusive water," Colwin's ideas included, but for now the main take-away is that there is an application of force we must place against the water with our pulling arm.

FIGURE 3.1

ALLISON SCHMITT, 2008 OLYMPIC MEDALIST, REDUCES RESISTANCE AT THE SURFACE WHILE MAKING THE WATER SOLID BELOW.

REDUCING RESISTANCE

While the "hold" is taking place below us, our relationship with the water is completely different on the surface. The head, torso, hips, and legs should slip through the water. We do not want to feel like the water in front of us is solid. We have to move through it.

This is the part of swimming where we have been taught to think about body position and roll, head position, and any other technique that reduces resistance. While definitely important aspects of swimming, these techniques are purposefully neglected in this book. They are already being thoroughly discussed, and with too much emphasis, elsewhere. They are such hot topics that they are smothering any discussion of what really makes a swimmer competitive—the pull underneath.

THE VITAL ELEMENT REVEALED

There, the cat's out of the bag! Competitive swimming is far more about the pull than it is about body position. Take a sip of that Italian-roast coffee I hope you're drinking, and offer a toast to Pareto, because we have just revealed 80 percent of swimming!

If you don't believe me, then go to a beach and watch the sunbathers wade into the water and proceed to float on their backs, soaking in the warm sun. They have a wonderful body position on top of the water—as good as I did when I swam at the Olympics. The kicker is that they are not getting anywhere. Remember, swimmers need to move forward.

Now, don't misunderstand. Body position is definitely something that the top swimmers understand and try to perfect. Scientists, coaches, and swimsuit manufacturers all study the flow of water over and around the body, so I am not saying that this is not an important factor in swimming. What I am saying is that the most successful swimmers have worked to develop something that is far more vital—the pull. The only reason their work on body position means anything is because these swimmers are tearing up the pool already with an incredible pull.

PULL VERSUS BODY POSITION

I can sense the doubt from a few of you. You are just like a good friend of mine who is a top triathlete in his age group. He has been a student of the "glide like a fish theory" for a number of years and is very protective of it. He and I had a conversation during which he described a swim clinic he attended over a decade ago. By the end of the two-day clinic he was so convinced that swimming started and ended with body-position considerations only, that he actually believed the pull under the water was a fixed force. In other words, he believed that no matter what position he held his arm in, he was applying the same force, so to him the pull was a moot point. At the clinic, there was no discussion about the underwater pull. My friend believed his only potential for improvement was to reduce resistance, or as he put it, "to get his entire body to go through as narrow a tube as possible."

He said he had been working on this for more than a decade. When I asked him if he had become faster, he admitted, "Well, no." The look I gave him said it all: You are one of the most intelligent guys I know, how in the world did you not realize something was wrong? The fact that he continued to work on something for more than a decade that resulted in no time reduction tells me that there is a need to help triathletes (and many masters swimmers and age groupers) see the real picture.

Books on the market today include every detail you would want to know about the swim stroke. They are full of great information, but none of them organizes the information to reveal the vital few. People who read those books are naturally going to gravitate to the aspects of technique that are most simple to apply. However, those aspects will not be beneficial if you lack the foundation of a solid pull.

I realize that I have to back up this claim, so let's get to that now. The following reasons explain why the pull is the vital factor and why body position is not.

Reason 1: Common Denominator Among the World's Best Swimmers

The pull is what the best swimmers have in common. When I studied underwater video and photos of the greatest swimmers throughout the past five decades, I noticed that the critical position of the arm under the water was virtually the same.

The world-record holders of the 1960s, 1970s, and 1980s were using the same crucial elements of the pull as the fastest swimmers do today. This, in and of itself, does not prove a thing. However, when combined with the fact that every triathlete and swimmer I know who struggles with going fast in the water is employing fantastic body-position technique yet none of the critical elements of the underwater pull, some conclusions can be made.

Why do we not see every serious swimmer and triathlete churning out a 57.4 in the 100-m freestyle like Johnny Weissmuller did? It is because Weissmuller knew how to "purchase" the water, as he said, and many athletes today have never given that a thought. Everyone is busy trying to get through that narrow tube my friend described. It is time to take a lesson from Weissmuller and figure out how to get ahold of the "elusive" and move forward.

If Weissmuller's time is not fast enough for you, then I'll step it up a notch. Let's look at Mark Spitz. He swam a 1:52 in the 200-m freestyle (long course) at the 1972 Munich Olympics. At the time, he was lugging around a big mustache and swimming in a nylon suit that is nothing like the space-age suits worn today. The pike dive, which essentially stops a swimmer dead in the water, was the rage, and there was no talk about "pressing the T" and "swimming downhill."

I could go on about how pool technology has improved and goggles were not allowed in 1972 and a number of other things, but hopefully the point has been made: You can try to get streamlined and reduce resistance all you want, but if you don't know how to hold the water beneath you and pull properly, then Spitz is going to crush you with his big, hairy mustache in tow, and Weissmuller is going to embarrass you even more as he sings his Tarzan song and strokes to victory with a technique that would mortify students and coaches of the "body position and glide" school.

Reason 2: The Law of Diminishing Returns

This law is one of the most famous in all of economics (sorry Pareto). It states that we will get less and less extra output when adding additional doses of an input while holding other inputs fixed. This law relates to our swimming situation in that once a swimmer is already horizontal in the water, then:

- We will get less and less extra output (i.e., faster swimming)
- When we add additional doses of an input (i.e., trying to get more horizontal in the water)
- While holding other inputs fixed (i.e., keeping the crummy pull fixed).

This is exactly what is happening in the triathlon world and much of the swimming world. Around 95 percent of the swimmers and triathletes I know (professionals included) are showing up to practice and working on diminishing returns.

How can this be? Why do so many people continue to work on elements of stroke technique that do not give them significant returns while completely ignoring the vital aspects? Though I can't be certain, I have a good guess as to how the story panned out.

Top swimmers and coaches have always searched for ways to get faster. Races are won and lost in increments of hundredths of seconds, so part of the study of swimming throughout the years has been to identify areas in which any gain, no matter how small, can be made. In the 1990s, body position became the new rage. I remember it clearly. I was swimming in Michigan with the Clarenceville Swim Club and rumor made its way across the country that a man named Bill Boomer was working with the Stanford swimmers on how to use the body core to improve swimming power, efficiency, and speed. It was mysterious to me; phrases such as "pressing the T" were being thrown around, and I had no idea what they meant. I just knew it was big stuff if Stanford was buying into it. Luckily, I was busy working on other glaring weaknesses, like not wimping out when my coach told me to swim 6 × 100 on 8:00 all out.

Anyway, an interesting thing happened at this time. While body-core concepts were being touted in the collegiate and club swimming world, a need, and thus a new market opportunity, for swim instruction was simultaneously growing within the triathlon and masters swimming world. Swim clinics began to sprout up around the country, and their focus was this new and exciting revelation about the body core and how to apply it to improve speed and power. Masters swimmers and triathletes signed up in droves, believing they were finally being handed the ticket to swimming prowess. Every other element of swim technique was virtually ignored, particularly the most vital one—the pull.

New information naturally breeds a flurry of enthusiasm. At some point though, a leader must emerge to tame the excitement. A levelheaded analysis requires that we understand how new information fits within the overall scope of our mission. Businesses and other types of organizations create mission statements and vision statements exactly for this reason—to guide decision-making and to be constantly reminded of the core of their existence. Otherwise, it is very easy to go astray, chasing rabbits. We have a limited amount of time, energy, and resources, so the majority of our work efforts had better be spent on activities that impact the bottom line.

This point was driven home in 2001 while I was touring a Mrs. T's Pierogie's manufacturing plant in Pennsylvania. As I stood in awe, witnessing thousands of pierogies streaming down the conveyer belt, I shouted over the noise of the machines to the president of the company, who was standing nearby, "This is a lot of pierogies! Do you make anything other than pierogies?"

His response, shouting back, was, "Well, one time we tried to make ravioli . . . but then we realized after a little while that we are just really good at making pierogies."

Mrs. T's knew the key to its success. The company tried something new, but it saw that the ravioli business was diverting too much energy and resources away from what made it successful.

With regard to your swimming, I assume that your vision or mission is to move forward, and at a pretty good clip at that. The core of your existence, if you are to be competitive in the sport, is time (remember *number of strokes × rate of turnover* from Chapter 2). Be careful not to chase rabbits (such as pursuing a reduction in stroke count without checking how it affects your time). Every choice you make needs to effectively support your vision.

The question then becomes, how do we know when new information supports our mission or diverts resources away from it? The answer: We will not know, or at minimum we will be taking a wild guess, unless we delve deeper into understanding all that is involved in the making of something. In other words, for you to take charge of your swimming goals and ensure that your efforts in the pool provide a certain level of return (rather than diminishing returns), you must understand what goes into the making of an authentic competitive swimmer. You must become what one of my favorite authors, Matthew B. Crawford, in his book *Shop Class as*

Soulcraft, calls a "craftsperson." Crawford, a motorcycle mechanic with a PhD in political philosophy, sways the reader to value the skills of the manual trades worker (i.e., plumber, electrician, mechanic) as much as the "soft-knowledge" skills of business executives. Among his many arguments—not the least of which is that the skills of the manual trades will never become obsolete—is that a craftsperson, because of his or her understanding of the production narrative (the details that go into the making of something), does not discard things that are perfectly serviceable in a relentless pursuit of the new.

In swimming, what if we all became craftspeople? If we really knew what went into the making of a fast swimmer—in other words, our "production narrative"—then our laps up and down the pool could be designed to effectively support any goal. We would know which elements of stroke technique impact the bottom line and which ones do not.

As mentioned in the Introduction, I want to show you the real picture of what the fastest swimmers do. I will endeavor to show you in upcoming chapters the production narrative so that your efforts in the pool provide you with a significant return rather than a diminishing return.

THE LEADERS IN THE CYCLING PACK FACE RESISTANCE, WHILE THE PELOTON TUCKS BEHIND.

Reason 3: The Theoretical Square Law

The implications of this law are found in many textbooks on swimming. The most practical explanation is found in *The Science of Swimming* by James Counsilman:

> *The Theoretical Square Law: The resistance a body creates in water (or any fluid or gas) varies approximately with the square of its velocity. To illustrate this fact, let us use an airplane going 100 mph and say that it creates 10000 pounds of resistance. When the airplane doubles its speed to 200 mph, it does not simply double its resistance; rather, the resistance increases by four times, or to 40000 pounds. If the plane increases its speed to 300 mph, it now increases its resistance by nine times. This law also applies to the swimmer's speed and resistance in the water. (Counsilman 1968, 16–17)*

The important word here is *square*. Remember from math class that squared means "to the second power." This is not the same as doubling. The theoretical square law is important to understand with regard to swimming, because it tells us that as we increase our speed, the resistance grows at an exponential rate, not simply at a rate proportional to the increase in speed.

This means that when a swimmer is traveling at faster speeds, then resistance becomes more of an issue. We have the quintessential chicken-and-egg question here: Which comes first, forward propulsion or reducing resistance? The answer is provided by the theoretical square law: Moving forward comes first. Only when we are traveling at greater speeds does resistance become an exponentially concerning factor.

Think about the Tour de France. When does the peloton break up and stay broken up? Not on the flat sections where the speed is fast, but rather in the mountains where the speed is slower. If we think about the theoretical square law in this situation, then it makes perfect sense. The cyclists leading the pack on the flat sections are traveling upward of 30 miles per hour in many places, and the resistance for them is massive. Every other cyclist can tuck behind the leaders and dodge the resistance. Once the mountains appear and the speeds slow down, however, the resistance for the leaders is much less. This is when strength becomes important, and when we see the best cyclists shine. Drafting no longer provides much advantage: the steeper the incline, the slower the speed, and the slower the speed, the less resistance the lead cyclists are facing (exponentially!). In the mountains, every cyclist is riding on a more level playing field, so to speak.

Going back to the theoretical square law as it applies to swimming: Reducing resistance becomes a relevant concern only if we are moving forward. Swimmers should invest their energy, focus, and time on developing elements of the stroke that first and foremost provide the propulsive forces. You should spend 80 percent of your time working on these propulsive forces. The top swimmers are doing this.

STILL SOME SKEPTICS?

No way! Some of you are still skeptical? Seriously? Even though we just finished talking about the theoretical square law and the law of diminishing returns, piero-gies, and everything else? Fine then, I am totally game for this drag-'em-down, knock-'em-out boxing match. Here are a few additional arguments to back up my claim that the pull is the most vital part of swimming.

FIRST, THE ONE-TWO COMBO

Our pull dictates both the number of strokes we take and the rate at which we take those strokes. No other part of swimming has a greater impact on those two factors.

NEXT, A LIGHT JAB

Think about the physical attributes of great swimmers. What is the most distinc-tive look of their bodies? It is the shoulders and the lat muscles; they have broad shoulders and distinctive V-shaped bodies, right? Well, common sense would tell us that if swimmers are meant to be most concerned with reducing resistance, then they should taper down those shoulders and lats a bit. Also, how did they get that look in the first place? Something tells me they did not get it from doing six-count extension and hip-rotation drills all day long.

THIRD, I'VE GOT MY OPPONENT AGAINST THE ROPES

You can get a great body position very quickly and with next to no physical effort. Remember those beachgoers floating on the water? Believe me, those vacationers are not stressing out trying to get that body position as they lie there on the water. In fact, most swimmers I have seen, whether age groupers, masters swimmers, or triathletes, have body positions worthy of an Olympic athlete. If the critical aspect of swimming fast pertained primarily to body position, then the whole world would be streaming through the water at great speeds, because everyone could develop it quickly and with little effort.

LAST, WATCH OUT, HERE COMES THE LEFT HOOK

If you are a triathlete, masters swimmer, or age grouper who has worked excessively on body position, and not on the pull, then I am willing to guess that your warm-up speed in practice is not much different from your main set speed. I see it all the time, especially in adults. They dive in for a warm-up and go a 1:27 on their first 100 yards. Then when the main set comes along, and they are supposed to be working hard at their repeat 100s, they crank out 1:30s. Ouch. That is not how it is supposed to work.

Great swimmers have a variety of speeds, including warm-up speeds, aerobic training speeds, threshold speeds, lactate speeds, and pure sprint speeds. They are able to vary their speed based on how much force they choose to put into their propulsion; it is not based on whether they choose to improve their body position on the threshold set more than on the warm-up.

This argument is winding down, but I still see one last bit of fight left in my skeptical opponent. I hear the rebuttal: "Come on! We cannot expect someone to swim with their feet dragging on the bottom of the pool." I say, fair enough. Allow those people the opportunity to address body position first. I'll concede that no one should have to struggle through the water vertically (nor should any observer have to suffer through watching that), but I give them one swim session to get it done. If it takes longer than that, then something is wrong. (Very new beginners, see sidebar on p. 35.)

The last point from my opponent is that the pull is too advanced to explain to new swimmers. I would say, "Oh, this is going to be fun. Please let me stand in the room when you tell them that."

TKO

Thank you for your patience while I debated my imaginary opponent. I am going to end this section of the book by saying that was a TKO and raising my own arm in the air (and I don't even like boxing). (For those of you who don't know what a TKO is, it is a technical knockout, and my opponent wants out of this bloody match.)

THE PULL: GOOD NEWS AND BAD NEWS

I only have a little bit of bad news: The pull definitely takes more effort, takes more time, and is more difficult to learn than any other aspect of swimming; this is partly why it is neglected at clinics. The position we must develop under the water does not simulate anything we do in life, so we are teaching a muscle memory that is completely foreign.

The good news is that it is not rocket science. It is 100 percent doable! Any swimmer who chooses to put forth effort on the pull will not only see improvement in swimming times but will also get toned, strong swimmer arms. If that effort is concentrated and nonwavering (in other words, if you keep it slow and easy for the first few weeks and do not bail out on stroke technique in order to keep up with your buddies in the lane), then you are going to see the first signs of improvement within three to six weeks. This is assuming you get to the pool at least three days a week (amount of yardage is not so important as long as every stroke is focused) and do the tubing exercises at least three days a week (these exercises are explained in Chapter 6).

FOR NEW SWIMMERS

For those of you who are new to swimming, or who have a natural aversion to the water, you will need to spend some time simply getting to know the water. Establishing the correct body position is easy, but learning to relax is sometimes not. Body position is important for you during this time, as is learning how to breathe. Work on keeping your head neutral in the water rather than lifting it (which many new swimmers do when they panic).

The great news is, while you are getting comfortable in the water for a few weeks, you can also train out of the water, developing your pull. This is explained in Chapter 6. The same chapter also explains one in-water exercise that will be very manageable for you. Then, once you feel comfortable in the water and are able to concentrate on technique, you will be ahead of the game in terms of strength, flexibility, and muscle memory.

1. **Swimming is a three-dimensional sport.** We have a job to do at the surface of the water where our body is moving forward, and we have a different job to do beneath us, in the third, deep-blue dimension where our arm is pulling.

2. **Beneath us the water must feel more solid.** We get a hold on the water with our hand/forearm to pull our body forward.

3. **At the surface, we must slip through the water.** We find ways to position our body to reduce resistance.

4. **Body position is important,** but it is not the separating factor between the best swimmers and those who struggle to go fast.

5. The **key to swimming fast**, above all else, is developing a great pull.

4

FLUID DYNAMICS & THEORIES OF PROPULSION

THE CHALLENGES & THE BEAUTY

By now you are surely convinced that the underwater pull should take its place as king of the hill in swimming. I know that once I started laying my bets on it, I made four Olympic teams. There is so much depth and potential in all that is below us when we swim, and I am excited that we are now nearing the part of the book that dives deep into this third dimension.

Before we get to the details that describe the pull and how to develop it, we have a little more foundational work to do; we will draw from it to make all the puzzle pieces fit. This final base layer of understanding requires that we revisit the topic of water, but this time from a scientific angle—particularly with regard to the study of fluid dynamics. Every textbook on swimming technique includes a significant piece on fluid dynamics as it relates to propulsion, and it is, without fail, the distinguishing topic that gives the book its reputation. Unfortunately, it is also the most laborious, scientific section of the book and for this reason holds the attention of very few readers.

STREAMLINING DEEP
IN THE THIRD DIMENSION

For a coach or athlete to grasp the concepts of "flow analysis," "vortex patterns," and "drag/lift forces" is no small task, so readers have a tendency to gravitate to sections of the book that are more manageable to understand (i.e., body position, hip rotation, head position). Since I have opened a can of worms by convincing you that the underwater pull is the most vital aspect of the stroke, I feel obliged to present the theories on swimming propulsion in terms that not only are understandable but also frame the sport on an entirely new level for you.

You are finally going to understand the origins of much of what you have heard from fellow athletes, coaches, and even that guy in the lane next to you at the health club who offers his two cents on how you should pull. If you have heard contradicting information, there is good reason; it is because the paradigms on swimming propulsion theory have shifted throughout the years. Often the swimming world would just be getting comfortable with one theory when another one would come along to take its place. This is due to the nature of the medium in which our sport is contested—water. Water complicates things. Cecil Colwin explains it this way in *Swimming Dynamics*:

What happens to the water when we swim? The answer is we don't exactly know....
Biomechanists claim to be able to calculate the forces that swimmers develop in the
water, but the trouble with these studies is that they depend on the premise of "essen-
tially still water." Water doesn't obediently stand still while forces act upon it. Conse-
quently, some studies may well be flawed because they are based on the mechanic of
solids rather than those of fluid behavior. (Colwin 1999, 72)

Colwin continues: "Moreover, prominent fluid dynamicists, when asked whether the flow reactions to human swimming propulsion could be analyzed by computer simulation, expressed the opinion that the rapidly changing body configurations of human swimmers almost defy complete analysis" (p. 78).

What does this mean for us? It means that we take this understanding that a human being moving through water is a bugger to analyze and put that understanding in our back pocket as we read about the four main theories of propulsion that have prevailed, at one time or another, during the past 50 years or so. Below is a short synopsis of each.

THEORIES OF PROPULSION

Newton's Third Law, Pre-1960s

The first and most logical explanation of what was taking place under the water centered around Newton's third law: for every action there is an equal and opposite reaction. Swimming theorists believed, prior to the 1960s, that the arm and hand acted as a "paddle" that pulled straight back, with the equal and opposite reaction being that the swimmer moved forward. Simple enough. It makes perfect sense.

Or does it?

The S Pull and Bernoulli's Principle, 1960s to 1990s

In the 1960s, James "Doc" Counsilman (coach of Mark Spitz at Indiana University and the man credited with being perhaps the most pioneering mind in swimming history) noted that the hand does not take a path straight back; rather, he showed that the great swimming champions employed a pattern that looked like an inverted question mark. Many of us know it as the "S" pull.

Newton's third law for swimming propulsion theory was subsequently scrapped, and the argument was made that the inverted question mark pull was a more logical explanation due to the nature of fluid dynamics. Essentially, the theorists claimed that the arm could not simply pull or push straight back, because once the swimmer's hand/arm (the "paddle") began to apply force, the water moved. Once the water moved (as the paddle progressed through the length of the stroke), then less and less force could be applied upon that already moving water. In essence, they argued that Newton's third law stood true when considering forces applied to a solid, but not so much when applied to a fluid.

Counsilman theorized that the swimmer must constantly search for new, "still" water in order to effectively apply force, thus the sculling movements of the S pull became the focus of research. Both Counsilman and a gentleman named Ernie Maglischo literally wrote the books on this new discovery, likening the effect of the sculling motion to an airplane propeller and wing. In Maglischo's book *Swimming Faster*, published in 1982, and in Counsilman's book *The New Science of Swimming*, published in 1994, there are detailed explanations of lift forces, drag forces, and Bernoulli's principle of fluid dynamics.

Cecil Colwin, in *Swimming into the 21st Century*, also acknowledged the discovery: "Counsilman's study showed that, in all the swimming strokes, the pull does not follow a straight line but is composed of short sculling motions, or impulses, that change direction as the hand moves in a curved path across the line of a swimmer's forward movement" (Colwin 1992, 20). However, while Colwin agreed that the hand does indeed take a curvilinear path rather than a straight line, he published his own theory for why this sculling motion provides forward movement and how the swimmer is to manage it.

The Vortex Theory, 1990s to Present

Colwin introduced to the swimming world the concept of the vortex (see Figure 4.1). What is a vortex, you ask? I asked the same question. Luckily for us, Colwin describes it quite well in his book *Swimming Dynamics*:

FIGURE 4.1

A SERIES OF VORTICES PRODUCED BY A SWIMMER'S KICK

A vortex is a mass of fluid that rotates about an axis. . . . A vortex is a form of kinetic energy, the energy of motion. A shed vortex represents the energy produced by a swimmer and "given" to the water. In fact, when you see vortices produced by the swimmer in the water, you are actually looking at the swimmer's propulsion. . . . Vortices often become visible to the underwater viewer when a swimmer is moving at top speed and accidentally entraps air into the stroke.

In 1984, I presented a study on the significance of vortex flow reactions in the swimming stroke. Later I was surprised to hear my report referred to by biomechanists as the "vortex theory of propulsion." This is not a theory but a physical fact—there exists no other way of producing propulsion in a fluid.

Without the resistive friction provided by vortex turbulence within a fluid, no tractive force would be provided. This is as true for swimmers as it is for ocean liners. In fact, all forms of propulsion through a fluid, whether by airplanes, fish, birds, flying insects, and so on, depend on resistive forces provided by vortices. (Colwin 1999, 74)

Colwin ultimately pioneered a worthy explanation of swimming propulsion by connecting vortex science with his observations from the pool deck. His work yielded an interesting description of how a swimmer should feel for the flow of water at various phases of the stroke, and he explained how the swimmer becomes a skilled "shaper of the flow."

Newton's Third Law (with Diagonal Components), 2000s to Present

Finally, the most recent text comes from Maglischo, and in it he backpedals to the 1960s. In *Swimming Fastest* (2003) he retracts his own theory from 1982 that was published in *Swimming Faster* (which used the airplane propeller and wing, lift, drag, and Bernoulli's principle to explain the success of the sculling motion). The reason for the retraction? The point was made that a boundary layer is present on airplane wings that is not present on the human hand and arm, and this boundary layer is critical for Bernoulli's principle to apply. Therefore, the explanation that the human hand and arm together act in the same way as an airplane propeller or wing could not hold up.

The following is Maglischo's retraction and his comments on Colwin's vortex theory of propulsion:

> I now believe that some of the information I presented on stroke mechanics in previous editions was incorrect. My primary purpose with this edition is to correct that information.
>
> I consider the evidence that Bernoulli's Principle is not involved in swimming propulsion quite compelling. I also believe that the evidence currently available does not support the notion that propulsion is the result of forming and shedding vortices. In my opinion, Newton's Third Law of motion, the law of action-reaction, offers the most likely explanation for human swimming propulsion. (Maglischo 2003, Preface)

Maglischo goes on to state, "I believe that the act of pushing water in a predominantly backward direction creates the propulsive force that accelerates a swimmer's body forward" (Maglischo 2003, 18). The key word in this sentence is *predomi-*

nantly. Maglischo does not boomerang all the way back to the pre-1960s theory that subscribed to Newton's third law. He believes there is a presence of lift and drag forces still in play and that the backward push has a diagonal component to it.

Stay tuned for the latest though. Maglischo learned from his past mistake, and this, combined with the fact that how water reacts when we pull is not completely understood, led him to make a disclaimer in *Swimming Fastest*: "While this is the theory of propulsion that I have come to accept after several years of study, I cannot guarantee that it is, in all respects, an accurate explanation of human propulsive mechanisms. At the present time, however, it seems to be the most logical explanation based on the available evidence" (Maglischo 2003, 18).

Despite Ernie's disclaimer and the recognized limits of scientific analysis in general, each theory described above contains numerous key insights—insights we can take to the pool. We will grab bits and pieces from the great work that Maglischo, Counsilman, and Colwin have done to craft a beautiful, powerful swim stroke.

1. Scientists are not yet able to fully analyze the **propulsive forces** of a swimmer.

2. The **four main theories on swimming propulsion** that have prevailed at various points during the past six decades include principles centered around:

   a. Newton's third law: Push straight back to move straight forward.

   b. Lift, drag, and Bernoulli's principle: Employ an "S" pattern to find still water.

   c. Vortex theory of propulsion: vortex turbulence within a fluid provides resistive friction. Shape the flow of water.

   d. Newton's third law with a diagonal component: Push back with a diagonal component.

3. Each theory provides **clues about how to work with the water** to gain the propulsive power you need to be the best swimmer you can be.

THE UNDERWATER PULL
VITAL ELEMENTS OF THE VITAL ELEMENT

We are building something here, and the foundation has just been laid. Each one of us, no matter what our goals in swimming, should have a firm grasp of the big picture and the choices that can be made. Understanding fluid dynamics, theories on propulsion, and the rate/stroke equation provides a solid footing from which to build the best swim stroke.

With the big picture now in hand, you are ready to look closely at the underwater pull and learn the vital elements of this vital element. Yes, you read that correctly—there are vital elements to the vital element.

One truth here is that technique cannot be boxed. Individuals have unique levels of strength, flexibility, and other attributes, including a natural rhythm. For instance, Ian Thorpe of Australia—Olympic champion in the 400-m freestyle in 2000—was so strong in his upper body that he could begin the critical elements of the underwater pull with his arm fully extended. Brooke Bennett, on the other hand, the women's gold medalist in the 400-m freestyle at those same Olympics, swam completely differently; her stroke was short and choppy, and her arm never came close to extending before she got ahold of the water below. If you look at

FIGURE 5.1

A WELL-FORMED HIGH-ELBOW POSITION IS KEY TO YOUR PULL.

10 different swimming champions you will see variances in the stroke mechanics in each one of them; however, without fail, they all eventually make their way to the critical elements.

My goal has been, and continues to be in this chapter, to give you an understanding of the things you cannot do without. Once you know those few things, then be brave—believe in your own style. Just never sacrifice the vital few. Every decision you make with regard to technique needs to support those critical elements.

THE FIRST VITAL ELEMENT OF THE PULL: THE HIGH-ELBOW POSITION

Some of the fastest swimmers in the world have awkward-looking recoveries, kicks, breathing patterns, and other quirks. They are, however, doing two things amazingly well. The first of these is the high-elbow position shown in Figure 5.1.

FIGURE 5.2 HIGH ELBOW ACROSS THE DECADES

MIKE TROY, 1960 OLYMPIC GOLD MEDALIST

MARK SPITZ, 1972 OLYMPIC GOLD MEDALIST

SHEILA TAORMINA, 1996 OLYMPIC GOLD
MEDALIST, SMALLEST SWIMMER TO WIN
OLYMPIC GOLD SINCE 1920

ALLISON SCHMITT, NCAA CHAMPION AND
2008 OLYMPIC BRONZE MEDALIST

Are you doing this? If not, then the rest of your pull is rendered virtually ineffective. The high-elbow position during the early phase of the stroke has always been one of the separating factors between champions and those who are stumped as to why their times are not improving. The underwater photos in Figure 5.2 span the decades, revealing how this critical element consistently shows up in the strokes of the top swimmers.

The high-elbow position was even present in Johnny Weissmuller's stroke. Although there are no underwater photos to prove it, Weissmuller writes a clear description of it in his book *Swimming the American Crawl*: "The upper arm should be raised, the elbow pointing upward to permit the forearm to hang down almost perpendicularly, and then go forward on a sort of pendulum swing" (Weissmuller 1930, 15). It's easy to see why he was able to post a 57.4 in the 1920s with a body position far less streamlined than any swimmer or triathlete today. He understood the high elbow (see Figure 5.3).

Two physical components are required for the high-elbow position: Strength and flexibility.

AN IMPORTANT NOTE
ABOUT THE HIGH-ELBOW POSITION

The high-elbow position takes place during the first third of the underwater-pull phase. In other words, swimmers are engaged in it during the "catch" phase, when they "purchase the water," as Weissmuller described it. The high-elbow position is not held the entire length of the underwater stroke. Once the catch is achieved and the swimmer's head passes over the forearm (approximately one-third of the way through the stroke), then the swimmer gradually begins the diagonal phase of the stroke that Maglischo describes. At the end of this chapter, we will discuss in more detail the diagonal and the finish of the stroke.

FIGURE 5.3 THE MECHANICS OF THE PULL

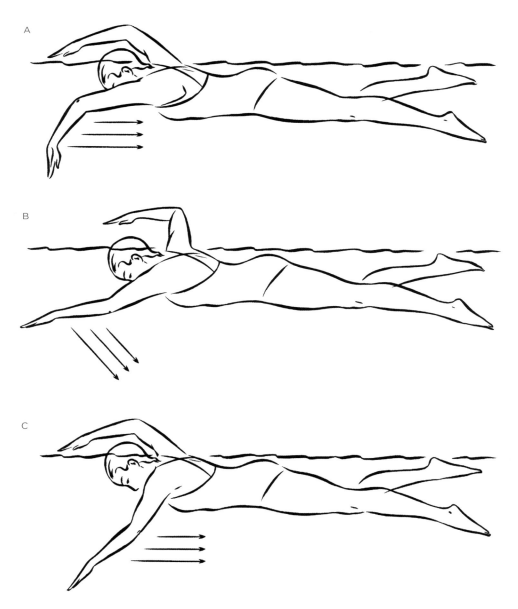

A HIGH ELBOW (A) IS KEY FOR A BACKWARD PRESS THAT MOVES A SWIMMER FORWARD.
A STRAIGHT ARM PLACES FORCE DOWNWARD (B), DELAYING THE BACKWARD PRESS (C).

Strength

As mentioned in Chapter 3, swimmers have distinctive V-shaped bodies and broad shoulders. Let's look at the broad shoulders first.

The reason most swimmers have broad shoulders is due to very well-developed deltoid muscles. The deltoid sits on the lateral side of the shoulder (see Figure 5.4.) It is the muscle that holds the upper arm high in the water, with the elbow pointing upward.

If you stand on dry land and hold the high-elbow position, the deltoid will quickly start to feel a burn. It is an extremely awkward position, unlike anything we normally do during our day; therefore, this strength is only developed with specific focus.

FIGURE 5.4

PETER VANDERKAAY, 2008 OLYMPIC GOLD MEDALIST, HAS THE WELL-DEVELOPED DELTOIDS TYPICAL OF STRONG SWIMMERS.

FIGURE 5.5

THINK OF THE ARM AS TWO LEVERS, THE UPPER ARM AND THE FOREARM/HAND.

To explain it a bit further, think of the arm as two levers (see Figure 5.5). The **first lever** is the upper arm, from the shoulder to the elbow, which during the catch phase (the first third) of the underwater pull is held high in the water (1–4 inches below the surface). The tendency is to drop the entire lever when fatigue sets in. Huge mistake! This is why we must stay focused and slow things down while we build this strength.

The **second lever** is the forearm that Weissmuller explained should hang down perpendicularly. The hand is also an important part of it. This lever (forearm and hand) is what "holds" the water. Each of the four theories on propulsion discussed in Chapter 4 acknowledges that the forearm and hand are responsible for the application of force that must be placed against the water. The theories diverge on the finer points of how to continually work with the water to maintain the resistive force, but they all promote that the hand and forearm hold the water.

The strength required to separate the two levers—to hold the upper arm high and then to bend at the elbow to engage a downward-facing forearm—must be trained. Finding this position is not natural, but it is critical that a swimmer be able to do it. If a swimmer does not separate the two levers, instead doing what comes easily and naturally, which is to initiate a press on the water either downward or to the side with a straight arm, then valuable momentum is lost. The correct use of the two levers is shown in Figure 5.3. Chapter 6 includes a variety of in-water and out-of-water exercises that will strengthen the deltoid and other muscles in the back and shoulders so that a swimmer may train the proper function of each lever.

Flexibility

The second physical component required for achieving a successful high-elbow position is flexibility. The high-elbow position during the early phase of the stroke requires that a swimmer not only be uniquely strong in his or her shoulders, but also uniquely flexible.

A responsive, strong muscle is not one that is tight and bound. If you look closely at the photos in this chapter, you will see a medial rotation of the shoulder against the chin and cheek area. This medial rotation occurs when the arm is fully extended in the water and throughout the first third of the stroke—the catch phase—and it is what allows the elbow to point upward. For years I took medial rotation for granted, believing it was simple to do. When I started coaching swim clinics, I was shocked to find the majority of people at the clinics could not rotate their shoulders toward their chin. It was then that I realized this movement had to be trained.

For this shoulder rotation to take place, the muscles surrounding the scapula (wing bone) must release to allow the upper arm (our first lever) to jut forward toward the chin. This movement gives a swimmer extension, or length of stroke. It is *not* a glide. "Extending" and "gliding" are two very different things. When an athlete extends, there is great dynamic energy; the core of the body tones and engages, or "turns on." In contrast, gliding is passive, lacking energy.

Look at the sequence of photos in Figure 5.6. They depict 1960 Olympic gold medalist Mike Troy in the front phase of the swim stroke. Note how the shoulder

FIGURE 5.6

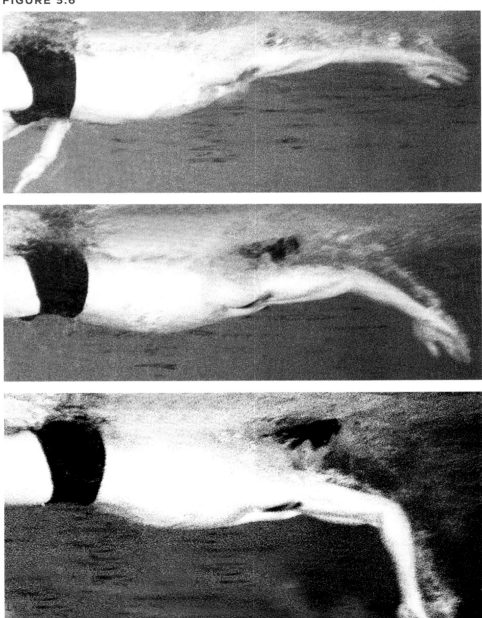

THE "CATCH PHASE" THAT HELPED EARN MIKE TROY GOLD AT THE 1960 OLYMPICS

is rotated next to the chin and cheek area (medial shoulder rotation). Also note the forward extension of the scapula (wing bone). Throughout the catch phase of Troy's stroke, the upper arm (first lever) is extended. The upper arm remains extended as he begins to bend at the elbow and purchase the water with his forearm and hand (second lever)—the high-elbow catch.

Chapter 6 includes exercises on how to develop the flexibility required for the high-elbow position. These will be difficult at first, but always remember that tissue does respond. If you keep working at it, you will see improvement.

SEATING THE HIGH-ELBOW CATCH

Some swimmers, when they first hear about the high-elbow position are so enthusiastic that they try to hold the upper arm too high during the catch phase ... so high that the upper arm comes out of the water. Remember that more is not always better. A swimmer does not gain anything if the arm comes out of the water. To hold water, our limbs must be seated in the water (see Figure 5.7). Note that the elbow sits approximately 1–4 inches below the surface of the water as it points upward and outward during the high-elbow catch.

But also take note that the high-elbow position is not an all-or-nothing athletic feat. Gradually build the position for more length, extension, and stabilization. If you are new to swimming, or new to focusing on the high elbow, your elbow position for catching the water will not need to be as dramatic as those of the Olympic swimmers in these photos. Seat your upper arm slightly lower in the water to start. You will still be making great gains on holding water even if the elbow is an inch or two lower than these photos show; however, always be sure that the second lever (the hand/forearm) hangs down perpendicularly from the upper arm. This is what it truly means to have a high-elbow catch. The degree and strength of the catch will be built throughout a season and even a full career. Chapter 6 provides exercises and drills to build this strength.

FIGURE 5.7
PETER SEATING THE HIGH-ELBOW CATCH

THE SECOND VITAL ELEMENT OF THE PULL: HOLDING THE WATER

Developing a hold, or "feel" for the water, is the second vital element of the pull and one of the most beautiful and rewarding parts of swimming. Feel has everything to do with the forearm and hand, fluid dynamics, propulsion, and the application of force against the "elusive."

A feel for the water is said to be the gift of only the talented. Not so. It belongs to any person who is thoughtful and patient, like a craftsperson or an artist—someone who is willing to put aside the sales pitches in order to study and understand what real swimmers have mastered.

This is our tao, our method, our way. Scientists have sent rockets to the moon, but they are at a loss to definitively say how our bodies are sent to the other side of the pool. How could we, therefore, come to any other conclusion than that this aspect of propulsion is one of the critical, separating factors in our amazing sport?

While we may approach the high-elbow position in a mechanical way (it is a function of strength and flexibility), this element of feel has no tolerance for science, mechanics, or reasoning. It is a swimmer's sixth sense, a strange cousin to the normal sense of "feel" with which we are all familiar.

The theories on propulsion reviewed in Chapter 4 provide wonderful clues as to what this sense of feel entails. Which strikes a chord with you? I find parts of each valuable.

Cecil Colwin, in his vortex theory of propulsion, thoughtfully describes how the energy produced by a swimmer is "given" to the water. He makes us want to look for our own vortices—the columns of kinetic energy we produce, which are visible if air is entrapped by the propulsive limb. I tried to see the vortices from my kick once and almost threw my neck out as I swirled around to look back. Not recommended.

However, what about wrapping our minds around feeling the "resistive friction" and "tractive forces" that Colwin shares with us? It would be a massive mental shift, perhaps, but what if you stopped thinking about reducing resistance for a while and started thinking instead about increasing resistance for the sake of traction? The top swimmers are doing this (see Figure 5.8).

Give it some consideration. Your greatest breakthroughs will come when you bravely step away from your comfort zone and old habits.

Doc Counsilman taught us to steer away from the moving water that is continuously created throughout the pull. He said that a swimmer must search for still water. Where is that still water, you may ask? Well, it is not too far away; you need not do a far-sweeping S-pull pattern searching for something that is right in front of you. Only two to three diagonal sculls, or "impulses," from the hand and forearm are necessary. Impulses are slight angle changes made by the hand and forearm as they press back on the water.

Please note that a feel for the water, and the diagonal impulses, must take you in a *forward* direction. Be conscious of this. You may be in the water feeling the resistive forces like a champ, but if they are not applied in such a way as to move you forward, then you are no better off than before you started reading this book.

Your craftsmanship is the best way to master a swimmer's feel, and Chapter 6 includes a sculling drill to introduce the concept of pressing or impulsing on the water.

Ernie Maglischo must have realized that people were taking the S pull a bit too literally, sweeping laterally with such great effort that they threw common sense

FIGURE 5.8

ALLISON, IN THE DIAGONAL PHASE OF HER PULL, INCREASES RESISTANCE FOR THE SAKE OF TRACTION.

(the need to move forward) right out the window. Now he chooses his words more carefully: "I believe that the act of pushing water in a predominantly backward direction creates the propulsive force that accelerates a swimmer's body forward" (Maglischo 2003, 18). Does this description connect with you better because of the simplicity? What could be more simple than envisioning your hand and arm pushing backward? Perhaps Maglischo believes the swimmer will naturally make the scull impulses required to find the still water. He may think that overdescribing a sculling component is more risky than underdescribing it, knowing that humans have the tendency to think more is better.

If you identify with Maglischo's description, just remember that he says "a predominantly backward direction" not "a completely backward direction." You will be swimming like a stiff wooden paddleboat if you do not incorporate some intuitive impulsing.

As for me, I find inspiration in all of the above. I also believe that envisioning a wall underneath you is helpful. Take care not to picture that wall too low beneath you, because that might cause you to drop the upper arm too low in the water.

FIGURE 5.9

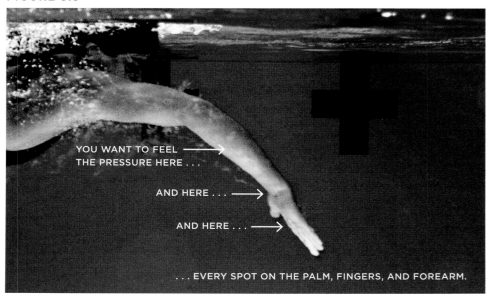

YOU WANT TO FEEL THE PRESSURE HERE . . .

AND HERE . . .

AND HERE . . .

. . . EVERY SPOT ON THE PALM, FINGERS, AND FOREARM.

THE THREE PHASES OF THE PULL

Figure 5.10 illustrates the three phases of the pull. While studying this diagram and the photos that follow, look closely at each phase of the stroke. The diagonal (2) and finish (3) phases of the underwater pull are as important as the high-elbow phase (1). The content of this book is heavily weighted toward the high-elbow catch phase, because it is the most physically awkward and demanding phase of the underwater pull, thus the least likely to come naturally to a swimmer. However, in order to continue momentum in the water, swimmers must create forward propulsion throughout the length of the underwater pull; the diagonal and finish phases, although much less mechanically awkward, are as important as the high-elbow catch phase and include critical details.

Remember, the entire upper arm (our first lever) must be raised, with the elbow pointed upward. Our imaginary wall sits high in the water, perhaps only a foot or two below the surface, in order for our hand and forearm to grab hold of it.

The words I always say to myself while swimming are "pressure on the water." This pressure is something you want to feel in every nook and cranny of your palm, fingers, and forearm. Every nook and cranny!

The wrist should be flush (straight) with the forearm so that you feel the pressure even in the crease between the forearm and palm. If you have a bend in the wrist, then you are missing an entire section of surface area where you should be feeling the water. Look at the photo in Figure 5.9. Once the swimmer has caught the water and has a high elbow, the wrist is flush. The arrows show the places where you want to feel pressure.

While it is no problem to point arrows directly to the mechanics of the high elbow, pointing directly to "feel" is not so straightforward. However, a look at the full pull sequences and photos of top swimmers on the following pages will teach you more about feel than words can describe or arrows can show.

FIGURE 5.10 THE THREE PHASES OF THE PULL

THE CATCH (1), THE DIAGONAL (2), THE FINISH (3)

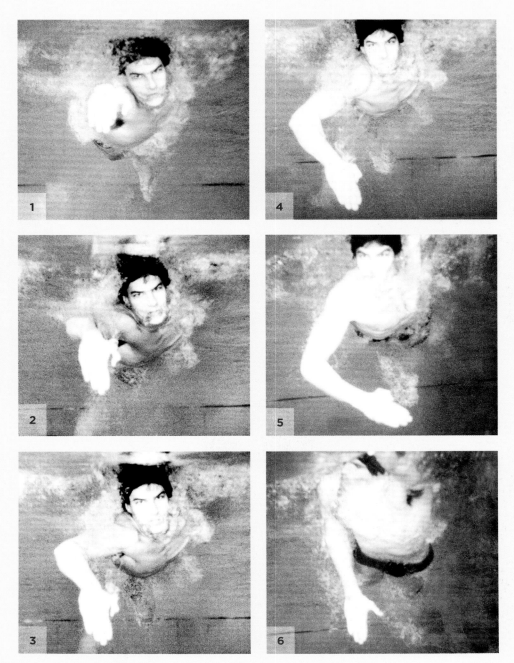

MARK SPITZ, 1972 OLYMPIC GOLD MEDALIST

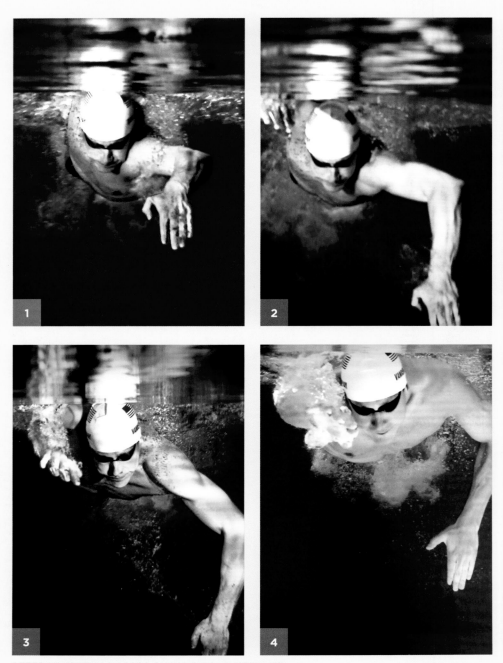

PETER VANDERKAAY, 2008 OLYMPIC GOLD MEDALIST

ALLISON SCHMITT, 2008 OLYMPIC BRONZE MEDALIST

CLOSER LOOK AT THE FULL LENGTH OF THE PULL

1. Hand Position and Tone

The palm of the hand is held open and flat, rather than cupped, in order to maximize surface area. Hold fingers straight and together with tone. "Tone" implies a strong form; it is neither too rigid nor too relaxed. Many top coaches agree there should be no more than 20 lbs. of tension in the hand/forearm muscles. Any more than this causes too much rigidity in the muscle tissue, thus affecting the swimmer's ability to intuitively feel the water. If you hold the hand and fingers correctly, with tone, there will be a slight, slight (did I say "slight?") space between each finger, which creates a boundary layer. The boundary layer has a weblike effect that helps us to feel (and hold) more water. Feel the water on every point of the palm and fingers, even on the sides of the fingers where you have created a boundary layer.

Remember that the high elbow is employed during the first third of the stroke only, but feeling (holding) the water is a critical factor throughout the length of

FIGURE 5.11

KEEP HAND TONE ALL THE WAY TO THE FINISH.

the underwater pull, from the high-elbow catch through to the diagonal (middle phase) and the finish (last third of the stroke).

Hold your hand tone throughout the length of the stroke (see Figure 5.11). Do not "let go" of the water after first catching it in the high-elbow position; hold the water with hand tone throughout the diagonal and finish phases of the stroke.

2. The Paddle

The position and tone of the hand are critical for feeling the water, but the hand does not act alone. The forearm and hand act upon the water together as a paddle. The hand neither leads nor follows the forearm. The forearm neither leads nor follows the hand. From the catch to the finish, the hand and forearm (the second lever) act upon the water as one unit (see Figure 5.12). This increases the surface area so that the swimmer is able to hold more water. Having the hand and forearm act as one unit also engages the core muscles to help drive the body over the paddle, resulting in greater propulsive power and momentum.

FIGURE 5.12

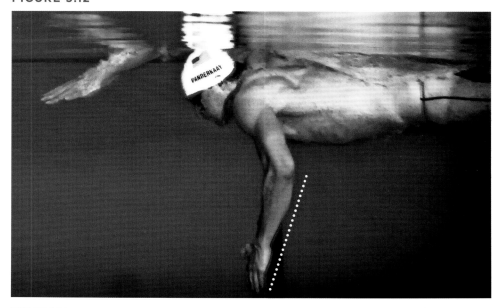

THE FOREARM AND HAND SHOULD ACT AS ONE UNIT ON THE WATER, ENGAGING THE CORE.

3. Position of the Hand and Forearm

Throughout the length of the underwater pull, the hand and forearm are positioned to place force *backward* against the water, even as the swimmer searches for still water with diagonal movements. (See Figure 5.13.) Examine the hand and

FIGURE 5.13

NOTE THE PITCH OF THE HAND THROUGHOUT THE LENGTH OF THE PULL.

forearm in every underwater photo of this book; they act upon the water together, always in such a position as to place force backward; they do not press laterally on the water as a sweeping S-pull pattern would.

4. Fingertips and Wrist Position During Catch

During the early phase of the pull (the high-elbow catch phase), fingertips point toward the bottom of the pool with a slight to no bend in the wrist (see Figure 5.14). If you bend the wrist during the high-elbow phase, then you lose the feel of the water in the crease where your forearm meets the palm. Also, bending the wrist brings a much higher risk of dropping the elbow unknowingly, thinking you are doing the mechanics correctly because the fingers point downward. With a straight, flush wrist, the only way your fingertips will point to the bottom of the pool is if you point the elbow upward and employ the high-elbow position.

FIGURE 5.14

MARK BEGINS TO FEEL THE WATER WITH A SLIGHT BEND IN HIS WRIST, BUT THE WRIST STRAIGHTENS AS HE ENGAGES IN THE HIGH-ELBOW CATCH.

5. Position and Stabilization of the Upper Arm Outside the Lateral Body Line

The high-elbow catch position establishes where the upper arm stabilizes (maintains it position) for the entirety of the underwater pull in terms of its position relative to the outside of the body. Even as the swimmer progresses into the middle and final phases of the stroke, the upper arm remains slightly outside the body, with elbow pointed outward. This position of the upper arm outside the lateral body line, with elbow pointed outward, is the position the upper arm first established in order to effectively catch the water in the high-elbow position. In other words, not only should the elbow be pointed upward during the high-elbow catch, but also it should be pointed outward, slightly outside the lateral body line, during this critical catch phase.

Swimmers who are accused of "crossing over" during the underwater pull are collapsing the elbow and upper arm inward toward the center of the body line (see Figure 5.15B). The lost stability in the shoulder and upper arm causes the muscles in the body core to disengage and results in less power from the stroke—a very costly mistake. The upper arm should never sweep inward or under the body during any phase of the underwater pull.

FIGURE 5.15

A CORRECT FORM   **B** INCORRECT FORM

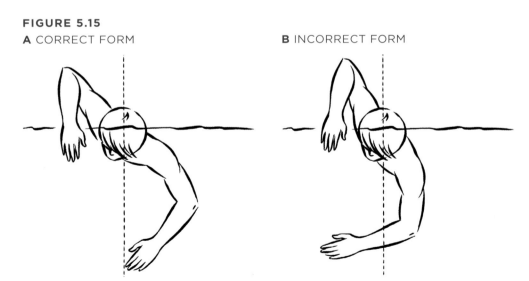

"CROSSING OVER" DURING THE UNDERWATER PULL, AS SHOWN IN B, IS A COSTLY MISTAKE.

FIGURE 5.16
MARGARET KELLY, SEVEN-TIME
NCAA ALL-AMERICAN,
SIX-TIME BIG TEN CHAMPION

LATS ⟶

So, although swimming is a dynamic sport, a great amount of stabilization takes place in terms of where the upper arm remains relative to the outside of the body line. Stabilization requires an *isometric* strength, which refers to having tension in the muscle without contracting. Holding water entails stabilization. Many athletes only feel satisfied that work is being done if their limbs are involved in a flurry of movement. It is difficult for some people to believe that stabilizing is key to achieving maximum power and speed.

Functional strength programs that incorporate stability exercises are more a part of top swim teams' training regimens than ever before.

The lat muscles in the back are one of the major muscle groups that come into play when holding the water, from the first moment of catching the water in the high-elbow position through to stabilizing the upper arm lateral to the body for the rest of the pull. The lats are part of the body core that pull the swimmer forward (see Figure 5.16). Ask any female swimmer if she enjoys shopping for a dress and she will tell you that it is nearly impossible to find one that zips up her back because of her lats.

6. The Diagonal Phase of the Stroke

Although the upper arm (the first lever) stays lateral to the body throughout the length of the underwater pull, it does angle approximately 45 degrees downward at the end of the catch phase of the stroke so that the body may begin to pass over the pulling arm. This downward angle of the upper arm begins the diagonal phase (the second third) of the underwater pull. (See Figure 5.17.) The diagonal movement is important both for moving the hand/forearm (second lever) onto still water and also so that the swimmer is in a strong mechanical position. Unlike the awkward position required for the high-elbow catch, this diagonal is a more simple and manageable mechanical position. It is important that it be done correctly, though, so that resistive friction on the forearm and hand is maintained and forward momentum of the core driving over the hand/forearm is continued.

7. Drive from the Core

Swimming propulsion is not solely based on the hand/forearm paddle applying force to the water; to reach maximum swim speed potential, there is another force at

FIGURE 5.17

ALLISON IN HER DIAGONAL PHASE

play—a core drive. If a swimmer holds the water properly, then the water in a sense becomes more solid (the swimmer is in a sense creating his or her own "wall" in the water below), and the hand/forearm lever is able to anchor onto the water. With this hold on the water, a swimmer should be able to envision the body moving over the hand/forearm rather than the hand/forearm slipping back. (See Figure 5.8.)

For the body to move forward on the surface of the water, there must be a dynamic drive from the body core. Look again at Figure 5.12, showing the tone in the core. I remind you that *body tone,* rather than body position, is a key factor to achieving propulsion and speed in the water. And always keep in mind that a core drive is impossible to initiate if there is no anchor point on the water; our pulling arm is our anchor point, and it all starts with the high-elbow catch.

Note in Figure 5.17 that as the body is passing over the hand/forearm, the forearm has the isometric strength mentioned in point number 5. You can see the pressure of the water against the forearm if you look closely at the muscle tissue; this indicates the hold on the water. Swimming propulsion is a marriage of two forces: (1) force from the pulling arm and (2) drive from the body core.

8. Hip Drive

Every body part is connected, from the hand and forearm that are anchoring to the core that is driving. There is a rhythm and chain reaction to the stroke. Hip drive is at play here. The hips are part of the core, and they work only as much as is necessary to help drive the body forward over the hand/forearm combination that is pressing on the water. Many swimmers erroneously believe that rotating the hips as much as possible is the key to swimming speed. Regard the hips as a *forward* driving force rather than a part of the body that rotates simply for the sake of rotating. Use the hips for dynamic energy, momentum, rhythm, and accentuation of the core drive. Momentum is gained when everything works together.

FIGURE 5.18

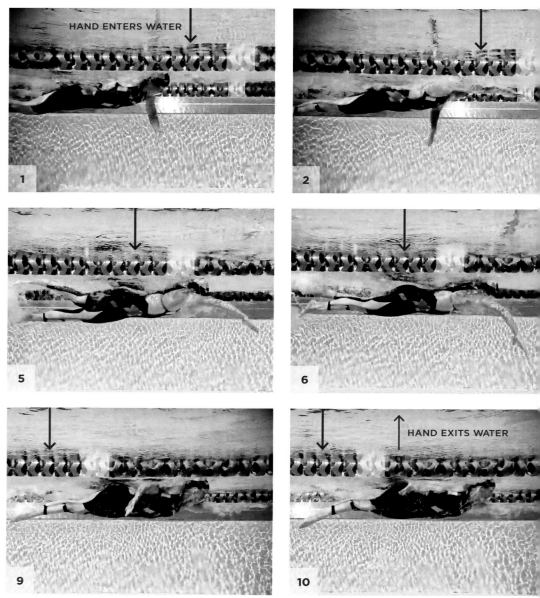

THIS SERIES SHOWS ONE STROKE CYCLE. THE DOWNWARD ARROW MARKS THE RIGHT HAND'S POINT OF ENTRY.

THE UPWARD ARROW IN FRAMES 10–12 MARKS WHERE THE RIGHT HAND EXITS THE WATER—
AHEAD OF THE POINT OF ENTRY—SHOWING THAT THE BODY MOVES FORWARD RATHER
THAN THE HAND SLIPPING BACK.

1. There are **two vital elements** to the underwater pull: a high-elbow position and feel for the water.

2. There are **three phases of the underwater pull**: the high-elbow catch phase, the diagonal phase, and the finish phase, all of which are equally important; but the high-elbow catch phase is the most awkward and difficult, thus the hardest for a swimmer to do naturally.

3. The **high-elbow position** is mechanical and relies on strength and flexibility. A swimmer employs the high-elbow position during the first third of the underwater pull—the catch phase—only.

4. **Feel is a critical factor** throughout the underwater pull, from the moment the swimmer catches the water in the high-elbow position through to the finish. Immerse yourself in this beautiful third dimension of our sport.

5. Scientists have yet to definitively explain the **propulsive forces** of a swimmer, but we can utilize the work of Maglischo, Colwin, and Counsilman to find clues as to how force should be applied upon the water to take us in a forward direction.

6. Much of the success of **mastering propulsion** comes from paying attention to finer details, such as hand tone, forearm and hand position, upper-arm position, and engagement of the core muscles that drive the body over the hand/forearm.

DEVELOPING THE UNDERWATER PULL

EXERCISES TO IMPROVE STRENGTH, FLEXIBILITY & FEEL

You have taken the path of least resistance for too long. I am going to toughen you up a whole lot, and you are going to love it! Soon you will be thanking me— perhaps not at first when your deltoids are on fire and your lats are so sore that you can barely lift your arms over your head—but soon you will be ecstatic that we crossed paths. You are going to come out on the other end a true swimmer.

This chapter includes the drills and exercises that, if applied with focus and attention to technique, will develop both your high elbow and feel for the water. If you are an adult who swims by yourself, then perfect. You will be able to fully concentrate on these exercises without interruption. For those who swim with a team, you may have to get creative with incorporating these exercises into the work-outs. The best way I know for doing that is to communicate respectfully with your coach. I had a fantastic relationship with my coach, Greg, for 30 years—from age 9 until my final Olympic swim at age 39—because we always shared ideas with each other (maybe not so much when I was 9). Work as a team on figuring out a plan to incorporate these drills and exercises.

The two vital elements of the pull (high elbow and feel) can be trained in the same session. Even considering the mechanical nature of one element and the sensitive nature of the other, it is possible to work the high elbow and the feel congruously. Some drills and exercises single out one element, while other drills work both critical techniques at the same time.

The drills and exercises listed in this chapter address strength, flexibility, and feel. Let's start with ways we can train the more mechanical of the two vital elements—the high elbow.

DEVELOPING THE HIGH ELBOW

1. Streamline

Streamlines are one of the most dynamic exercises for training muscle tone, explosiveness, and range of motion, including the flexibility required for a high elbow. Indeed, one of the most basic skills in competitive swimming is a streamlined push-off after the start and after turns. The benefits are obvious: a reduced resistance that allows the swimmer to take advantage of the propulsion generated by the legs from pushing off a solid starting block or a pool wall. Why then do a significant number of age-grouper, masters, and collegiate swimmers not take streamlining 100 percent to heart? I think many people take it for granted and believe it will be easy to do when race time comes. Not so. The flexibility required for a fabulous, effective streamline must be trained. It is an extremely strenuous position to develop.

Triathletes, you are not off the hook either. You may think it has nothing to do with you, since you usually contest your events in open water, but an athlete who passes up a streamline is passing up a free yoga workout off every wall.

If you choose only one thing from this entire book, choose this first exercise of streamlining. It is so simple, yet so neglected because of lack of understanding of all its benefits. You will gain the flexibility in the shoulder that helps you medially rotate your upper arm near your face and chin for the high-elbow position. Also, the lats and back muscles will gain strength and flexibility, thus allowing you to jut forward from the scapula as you grab water out front during your pull.

FIGURE 6.1

FOR A GOOD STREAMLINE, KEEP HAND ON TOP OF HAND AND REMEMBER TO SQUEEZE ELBOWS AND BICEPS INTO THE HEAD.

Note in Figure 6.1 that the swimmer has hand on top of hand and is squeezing the elbows and biceps into the head, near the ears—squeezing as much as possible! This motion takes great strength and resiliency at first. It is not natural. The tissue in the shoulders, lats, and triceps is stiff, and it is painful to ask it to stretch so much. In addition to the squeezing of the arms against the head, the body (core) is stretching as long as it can stretch and becoming strong, powerful, and toned, which will be a big player in core drive. The intercostal muscles, the abdominal muscles (including the internal and external obliques that we rarely consider), the transverse abdominal muscles, and the lats and triceps must be elongated to the point of feeling 3 inches taller. If you stretch and squeeze this much, then—and only then—are you doing a real streamline.

In addition to training the streamline each time you push off the wall during a swimming set, incorporate 10 explosive, power-packed, dedicated push-offs in which you hold as elongated a position as possible underwater for 4–5 seconds (you will travel approximately 5–10 yards) and then swim easy back to the wall for the next push-off. Once at the wall, take 15–20 seconds to rest and recover for a high-quality effort on the next repeat. Your tissue will respond beautifully, lengthening and toning, after a week or two of consistent effort.

A NOTE ABOUT TONE

Tone is a key benefit of streamlining. As stated earlier, beachgoers who float on the surface of the water have as good a body position as I had at the Olympics. Most swimmers and triathletes also have a body position this good. The part that is often missing, however, is body tone. There is a big difference between body position and body tone.

I learned about body tone through equestrian show jumping. When I started riding at age 36, my coach was appalled at my posture and told me to "sit up." I tried but was unable to maintain it. He said that I should be neither relaxed nor rigid. He used the word tone. Bingo. It registered. Tone was what I had developed in swimming by doing hundreds of streamlines each day. I had to take that same stretched-out strength and apply it to sitting up on a horse.

To be a strong athlete in any sport requires tone, which you can develop every day. Sitting up with good posture at your desk will strengthen the muscles of your core, front and back. Every push-off at swim practice also develops tone. When you run and feel fatigued, take note of your core posture. Are you hunching or elongating and maintaining a composed posture? It's good to push yourself to longer distances in training, but if you lose your posture and tone, then you are weakening, not strengthening.

2. Tubing and Halo Bench

The most dramatic gains in both flexibility and strength required for a high elbow are best accomplished out of the water. Developing feel is different; you have no choice but to be in the water for that. But for the high elbow you are at risk of being way off the mark if you work only on in-water drills, because water throws us off our rockers. Our perceptions of what we are doing in the water are often not even close to what we are actually doing.

The most logical place for working on strength outside of the water is in the weight room, and I am a big proponent of weight lifting and general strength exercises for swimming (and cycling, running, and triathlon, too). Unfortunately, there are no machines that fully simulate the high-elbow position in swimming. We can train the deltoids, triceps, and lats with various exercises, but not in the way we actually pull. Moreover, when we lift weights, we rarely work at a tempo pace. The Halo bench and tubing were specifically designed to train a swimmer's high-elbow position and tempo (rate of turnover, as discussed in Chapter 2). My advice is to do a strength program, and to make tubing training a part of it.

Look at Figures 6.2A and B and note the similarities between the position of the arm/hand training on the Halo with that in the underwater photo of the high

FIGURE 6.2

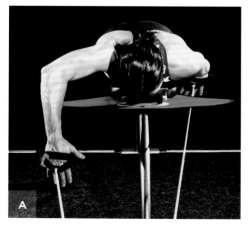

ARM/HAND TRAINING ON THE HALO BENCH

UNDERWATER PHOTO SHOWING
THE HIGH-ELBOW POSITION

elbow. How do you know if you are doing the tubing exercise correctly? The first clue is that your fingertips point toward the ground at the beginning of the pull. You must do this without bending your wrist. If you bend at the wrist, then you are able to achieve downward-pointing fingertips with a low elbow. Not good. You will be no closer than you were before to developing the high-elbow vital element.

Keep the wrist straight and flush with the forearm throughout the entire front phase of the stroke, as shown in Figure 6.3. Should the wrist have tone? You bet. Think of your wrist as neither relaxed nor rigid but, rather, as having tone.

The other key to proper technique when doing the tubing is to keep the upper arm raised and extended forward (jutting the scapula forward and medially rotating the shoulder toward the chin and cheek) during the first third of the pull-back. Do not allow that lever to drop at a downward angle until your paddle (the hand/forearm) has pulled one-third of the way back. One way to think about how to hold the upper arm during the first third of the pull is to keep the upper arm parallel with the ground. Another way to picture it is to keep your elbow the same height

FIGURE 6.3

REMEMBER TO KEEP WRIST STRAIGHT AND FLUSH WITH FOREARM.

as your shoulder (the purpose of the Halo template is to ensure this aspect). It will be obvious that you are doing this correctly if your deltoid muscle burns so badly that you are ready to cry uncle.

Once you have reached the one-third mark of the pull-back, the upper arm naturally angles 45 degrees downward with the elbow pointed away from the body, as discussed in Chapter 5. See the sidebar "Watch Your Form" on p. 89.

When I said at the start of this chapter that you were going to toughen up and no longer take the path of least resistance, the tubing training is exactly what I had in mind. These exercises will fire up your deltoids in 10–15 seconds, and your lats will be incredibly sore the next day. This is good though! The shaking in the muscles you will feel from tubing exercises *will* make you stronger. Too often we avoid pain because we associate it with "bad." A simple adjustment in perspective will help you endure the short amount of time you will feel the burning from the following sets. Stay strong. Stick with it. You will feel great within a couple of weeks.

The workouts on the following pages may be done with the Halo bench or with the tubing alone. In lieu of a bench, the tubing is easily hooked onto any anchored pole at a pool, such as diving boards, ladders, or backstroke flagpoles. But note that using the tubing alone requires that you regularly check to ensure

Tubing is the perfect replacement workout if you cannot make it to a pool to swim. It is easily packed in a suitcase and can be done in a hotel room, simply by attaching it to a door handle in your room. There are three levels of tension (resistance) from which to choose, from light to heavy. Most athletes benefit most with the medium level. There is no risk of hurting yourself if you use a tension that is a bit more than you are ready to handle, but the primary focus should be on technique. Choose a level of resistance that allows you to hold proper technique.

TUBING IS EASILY ATTACHED TO ANY ANCHORED POLE AT THE POOL, OR DOOR HANDLE IN YOUR HOTEL ROOM.

proper technique, since the Halo template is not present. If you are cognizant of this technique, then the physical benefits of the tubing-only setup are equal to that of the Halo-bench setup.

Figure 6.4 shows a full pull sequence, properly executed. For examples of improper technique, see Figure 6.5. The only thing that is imperative is that you concentrate fully on technique. When I was training for swimming before the 1996 Olympics, I pulled on the tubing four days per week for 14–15 minutes total pulling time each day. The sets varied from 3×5 minutes to 7×2 minutes. I simulated my

FIGURE 6.4

FULL PULL SEQUENCE ON HALO BENCH WITH HALO TEMPLATE

200-m freestyle goal for tempo and number of strokes when I did 2-minute repeats. I did this after my evening swim practice, and rested for 2 minutes between sets. This is quite a bit of tubing exercise. It is not necessary to do this much if you are a triathlete juggling the training demands of three sports.

As a triathlete, I lessened the amount of tubing training due to energy and time constraints, but it was still a critical part of my swim strength and conditioning plan. During these years, tubing training entailed three days per week for 7–8 minutes pulling time each day. Sets varied from 7×1 minute, to 4×2 minutes, to 5×1.5 minutes, with a rest period equal to pulling time.

Remember: The Halo bench and tubing simulate only the underwater portion of the swim stroke. Do not recover your arm over your head as you would do while swimming. The tension on the tubing is too much for the shoulder. The correct technique for recovering the arm back to the starting position is to take the same path—but reversed direction—on the recovery that you took when pulling back.

FIGURE 6.5 IMPROPER TUBING TECHNIQUE

THESE TWO PHOTOS SHOW A DROPPED ELBOW AND A BENT WRIST. ALWAYS CHECK THAT YOUR ELBOW IS HIGH AND YOUR WRIST IS STRAIGHT/FLUSH BEFORE PULLING BACK.

THE WRIST IS STRAIGHT BUT THE ENTIRE FIRST LEVER (UPPER ARM) HAS BEEN DROPPED. ALWAYS CHECK THE HEIGHT OF YOUR ELBOW BEFORE PULLING BACK.

FIGURE 6.6

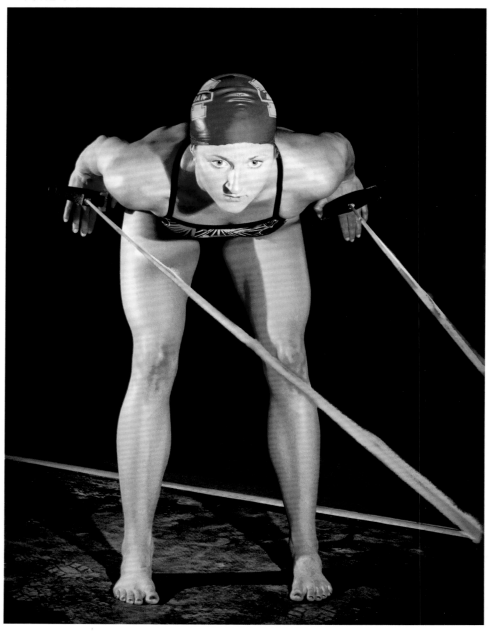

MARGARET DEMONSTRATES THE FINISH PHASE OF THE STROKE.

WATCH YOUR FORM

The one-third point of the pull is when the hand/forearm paddle passes under your head and shoulders and begins the middle third of the pull. During the middle third of the pull-back, be sure the forearm and hand act as one paddle, imagining water pressure on the entire paddle; this will keep the core and lat muscles engaged. Also, remember to keep the upper arm stabilized in relation to its position outside the body; the elbow and upper arm never collapse under the body during any phase of the pull-back, especially during this middle third. Finally, be sure to finish the last third of the pull near your hip rather than wide and out (see Figure 6.6). Look at Figure 6.7 showing the underwater stroke and note where the hand is finishing. It is brushing the hip just as Figure 6.6 depicts with the tubing.

FIGURE 6.7

WHETHER UNDERWATER OR DURING DRY-LAND EXERCISES, THE HAND SHOULD FINISH NEXT TO THE HIP.

WEEKS 1–2

Do the following three days per week: 3 × 8 repeats on each arm. Technique is everything. Start with your arm in the high-elbow position. Stop! Hold it there. We are not working tempo at this point. Check the following before pulling back slowly:

1. Fingertips point downward.
2. Wrist is straight and flush with the forearm.
3. Upper arm is parallel with the ground (or check that your elbow is the same height as your shoulder).

Ensure these three technique points before every pull-back. Remember to recover back to the starting position with your hand/arm low, taking the reverse path you took on the pull. Do not recover as if you were swimming in the water.

WEEKS 3–4

Do the following three days per week. Technique is still the most important factor (it always will be). You should be starting to feel more comfortable with the position. Everything is the same as weeks 1–2, but now try 3 × 12 repeats with each arm. Be sure to check your position before pulling back.

Try leaving your comfort zone just a bit by feeling the tissue of the upper lat (that attaches into your armpit area) extend. You will be jutting the scapula more and trying to medially rotate your shoulder near your face/chin. Small gains in range of motion make a big difference in athletic performance, so push just slightly out of your natural range.

WEEK 5 AND BEYOND

Only you know if you are ready for more or need to stick with a concentrated slow technique. If you are correctly establishing the high-elbow position more naturally and quickly at the start of each pull, your tissue is responding to the consistent training. The next section offers suggestions for progressing. Promise me you will never sacrifice proper technique for a hammerhead mentality, OK? Thank you.

Train in time increments rather than a set number of repeats. Do sets of 30 seconds, 45 seconds, or 1 minute. Build up the number of sets you do. Start with 3 sets and increase to 6 sets as the weeks progress.

Do two arms at a time, or stay with an alternating one-arm freestyle rhythm. If you choose to pull back with two arms simultaneously, then you are doing the butterfly pull pattern. The butterfly pull pattern is the same as freestyle when doing tubing, from the high-elbow catch to the finish. The workout in the arms is the same; the difference is that your core will have to work slightly more to reach for the high-elbow catch during the butterfly two-arm than it does on the freestyle one-arm. I like to alternate sets, half butterfly and half freestyle.

Incorporate tubing into your swim workout. Once a week plan a swimming set within your overall workout in which you alternate a swim repeat with a tubing repeat. For instance, choose 6 × 100 freestyle, and after each 100 yards (meters), press out of the water and do either a 15-second, 30-second, 45-second, or 1-minute pull on tubing, depending on your level of strength. Take approximately 15 seconds of rest before getting back in for the next 100. The goal for your 100 freestyle swim is to keep great form. You will be fatigued in the deltoids, lats, triceps, and core muscles. Maintain your composure and tone. You may do the 100s for form only, or you may decide to include a fast 25 at some point as a challenge.

Add in an exercise that isolates the triceps. This will add variety and provide additional strength. For example, if you do a 30-second repeat on the tubing, add a short spurt of tricep isolation at the end, for approximately 10–20 seconds. The tricep isolation is simply the back finish of your stroke. It burns tremendously but has great benefits. This is a very short, quick motion. Look at the photographs in Figure 6.8 to understand the short range of motion in this exercise. Also note that

(Continued on page 92)

(Continued from page 91)

the fingertips are always pointing downward and that the upper arm remains stable against the side of the body the entire time during this exercise.

Train your tempo for a specific race. As mentioned, I trained my 200-m freestyle strategy (tempo) out of the water with tubing almost as much as I did in the water. You should know your goal tempo. If you do not, then work with your coach on this. If you swim alone, then ask a friend to go to the pool with you and time your rate. Training turnover rate (tempo) on tubing is ideal. Chapter 7 explains and reviews the top swimmers' tempos.

FIGURE 6.8

  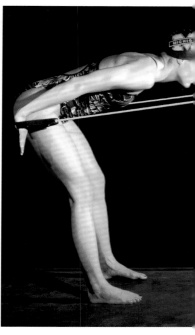

MARGARET SHOWCASES THE SHORT RANGE OF MOTION OF THE TRICEP ISOLATION EXERCISE.

FIGURE 6.9

WHEN DOING PRESS-OUTS, PLACE YOUR HANDS SLIGHTLY WIDER THAN YOUR SHOULDERS.

3. Press-Outs

The one thing in life that simulates the high-elbow position is pressing up and over walls. Train this movement simply by pressing up and out of the pool (see Figure 6.9). Notice if you take the vertical position of the press-out and transfer it to a horizontal plane, it's the same position as the high elbow we want to develop in our swimming.

For developing the high-elbow position, there's no better way than these exercises. If you do them faithfully, incorporating streamlines, Halo bench and tubing, and press-outs into your training routine, you will be as strong as Tarzan. But you are not ready to swim fast on that alone; you still need *feel*.

PRESS-OUTS

Incorporate sets of press-outs into your training. Do 3 × 10 after a workout, or make up a set similar to the alternating swim and tubing set described earlier: 6 × 100 freestyle, but this time do 5–10 press-outs after each 100 freestyle. Take 15 seconds of rest before pushing off for the next 100 yards (meters).

A set my coach had me do regularly was 10 × 50, pressing out after each repeat and diving in for the next 50 yards (meters). The interval was always tight, usually 40 seconds. I had to swim the 50 in approximately 30 seconds, which would give just enough time to press out, stand up, turn around, take a few breaths, and dive in for the next 50. By the end of 10, it is not so easy.

EXERCISES FOR DEVELOPING THE FEEL

As mentioned earlier, we must be in the water to develop a feel for it. There are no dry-land exercises that simulate the sensation of resistive forces against a fluid. In order to understand the very element that mystifies us, we had better jump in and become friends with it. The following describes five in-water drills that develop the feel.

1. Sculling

Sculling is the most important drill for learning feel. The best way to convey its importance is by the following true story.

In 1996, at our Olympic swim-team training camp in Knoxville, Tennessee, one week before the opening of the games, I was doing a 5,000-m workout with a few people on the team. Other teammates were in their lanes churning out workouts, but Gary Hall Jr., our top sprinter on the team, was standing on the deck in the sun. After soaking in the rays for a while, he decided to slip into the water in the lane next to me.

I was repeating 100s, and every time I came to the wall there was Hall, standing with the water chest high, never getting one hair on his head wet, sculling his hands back and forth in the water slowly and with great concentration. After 10 minutes he got out of the pool, and I heard him say to the coaches, "OK, I've got my feel for the water. See you later."

Hall won two gold and two silver medals at those Olympics, and he went on to make two more Olympic teams in 2000 and 2004, winning gold in the 50-m freestyle both times.

His entire workout that day was a sculling workout. He never went horizontal for a moment. I am not saying that all of us should do only sculling workouts from now on. First of all, Hall was tapering. Second, Hall is a sprinter, and sprinters are a different breed. Hall even falls into the category of being a different breed within the different breed (incredible talent and awareness). While I do not know how much he trained in terms of aerobic sets, endurance, sprinting, and weights, I do know that he did not get away with only sculling every workout, nor can the rest of us; however, we can deduce from this story that feel is critical and that sculling is a fantastic tool for training the feel.

Do 6–10 × 25 yards (or meters) of sculling, three times per week. The key is to feel pressure on various parts of the hand and forearm as you navigate the sculling movement. Make sure you feel the water along the entire lever, from elbow to fingertips, and not as much on the belly of the forearm as on the outer edges of the inside of the forearm. This sculling practice teaches us to impulse on the water so we understand what it means to press for resistive friction (a swimmer's feel) rather than simply going through a mechanical motion.

Even go so far as to think about areas that would normally be neglected, such as the outer edge of the thumb. Are you feeling pressure there? Do the same with the pinky. Do you feel pressure on that?

You may kick lightly while you scull, for coordination purposes. Do not kick so much that it propels you forward significantly. Your face should be in the water, lifting forward (not to the side) for a breath. Watch your hands and forearm, ensuring a high elbow, but mostly concentrate on your feel. You may also do sculling with a snorkel so that you do not have to lift your head for a breath.

Let's move on and describe the sculling motion and how to train it. There are many options. You do not necessarily have to get your hair wet. You can stand chest high in the water like Hall did and scull in a vertical position (perfect for beginners), but I recommend sculling while lying horizontally, as in the swimming position. This way you are able to work the high-elbow position while feeling the water. Look at Figure 6.10 to learn the sculling pattern.

The palms are turned outward at a 45-degree angle on the outsweep and then inward at the same angle on the insweep so that pressure is continuously placed on the water by the palm and inside edges of the forearm. This 45-degree diagonal pitch allows us to intuitively impulse on the water to master the feel top swimmers have developed. Keep the high-elbow position throughout the entire exercise. Keep the upper arm extended in front of you, jutting the scapula forward for an extended reach. The position of your arms should be just slightly wider than shoulder width,

FIGURE 6.10 THE SCULLING PATTERN

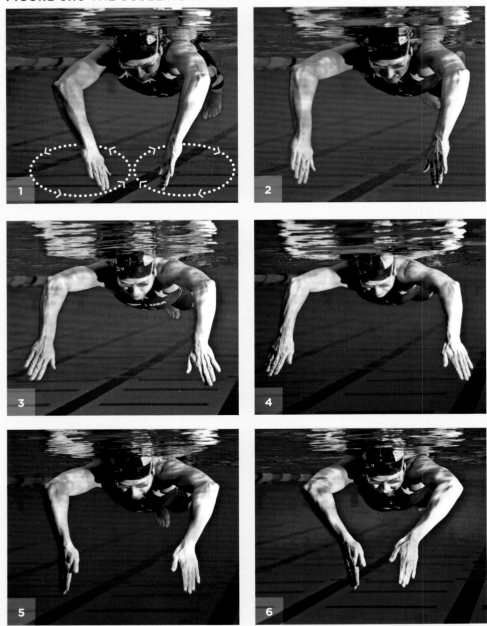

HANDS FOLLOW A FIGURE-EIGHT PATTERN AS ILLUSTRATED IN PHOTO 1.

with elbow pointed upward and outward. Look closely at the photos and note that the upper arm (lever 1, from shoulder to elbow) does not move; it remains stable. The sculling motion is taking place 100 percent with the forearm and hands, sweeping out and then sweeping back in.

2. Out-of-Water Recovery and Hand Entry

Detailed here is not so much a drill as it is normal swimming with a specific concentration (let's call it a drill anyway).

The purpose of this exercise is to set up the correct entry of the hand into the water. Many swimmers erroneously believe that reaching far out in front of their head and entering the water with the arm almost fully extended gives a longer distance per stroke. It does not. *Distance per stroke is determined by how far the body moves, not how far the hand reaches.* Not only does a far reach on the recovery not provide benefit, but it can actually cause problems, including the body going off balance, poor rhythm or timing of the stroke, a downward-pressing motion of the arm once in the water, and worst of all, a complete lack of feel at the most critical moment of the stroke, the entry.

I want to elaborate on this lack of feel at the critical moment of the stroke. Let's go back to Cecil Colwin's theory of propulsion in which he describes vortices and the concept of shaping the flow of water. Part of Colwin's advice to swimmers is to feel for the "oncoming flow" of water during the hand-entry phase of the stroke. If you watch the top swimmers, especially those who have longer strokes out front (*not* gliding strokes, but full-arm extensions), these swimmers enter their hand into the water just in front of their head (12–18 inches), and then, as the hand/arm extends, the entire second lever (forearm and hand) is *feeling* the water flow. These swimmers are, in a sense, becoming friends with the water, engaging in a relationship, as they extend. Once they are at full extension, they smoothly maintain that relationship and roll into their high-elbow underwater position.

Look at the two photos in Figure 6.11 of Allison Schmitt as she extends in the water before going into the high-elbow position. While it is easier to see a swimmer's search for feel during the in-water extension on slow-motion video, it can be seen even in still photos if you look carefully. These photos show the flow of water

FIGURE 6.11

NOTE THE SENSITIVITY IN ALLISON'S HAND AND FINGERS AS SHE EXTENDS IN THE WATER (A). ONCE SHE HAS REACHED FULL EXTENSION SHE MAINTAINS HER FEEL FOR THE WATER AS SHE MOVES INTO THE HIGH-ELBOW POSITION (B).

FIGURE 6.12

THE WATER CAN ACT AS A BED, AIDING YOUR HIGH-ELBOW POSITION.

around Schmitt's hand and forearm as she extends her arm before going into the catch. There is a great sensitivity that can actually be seen.

A swimmer who tries to reach out long in front before entering the hand and arm into the water misses the chance to feel the flow of water. They have missed out on sensitivity that will be vital once the underwater propulsion phase begins.

This drill is similar to two you may already know, the "zipper" drill and "fingertip drag" drill. Those two drills are equally acceptable to do as a replacement for this slow, concentrated swimming, but make sure that as you do them, you use those two drills to gain a sensitivity of the water that will flow into the high-elbow hold.

One other really neat thing to try to feel when doing this drill is the flow of water under your first lever (your upper arm, from shoulder to elbow). Remember that we want to keep this lever high in the water during the first third of the underwater pull (see Figure 6.12). If you concentrate enough, you will actually feel the water acting as a bed, aiding in holding up your upper arm. You should feel it in the armpit area, too. That is the underside of the upper lever, right? Utilize the water to hold up that entire underside part of your upper arm.

One last note: Since the out-of-water recovery is not a vital element of the swim stroke, you are at liberty to do whatever you want to do with it really. If it does not negatively impact the vital elements, then design it any way you desire. The most well known example of a stroke that incorporated a nontextbook recovery and entry

FIGURE 6.13

PRACTICE SETTING UP CORRECT ENTRY OF THE HAND INTO THE WATER WITH THE ENTRY DRILL.

Swim normally—but slowly—and once your hand in back finishes near your hip, begin the out-of-water recovery with a relaxed arm. Lead with the elbow. Your elbow should lift as if you were a puppet being directed by a puppeteer. Only lift the elbow; your forearm should dangle, relaxed as shown in Figure 6.13. In fact, on this swimming drill, shake out your hand and fingers as you recover. That is how relaxed you should be. Once your forearm/hand recovers, enter your hand into the water 12–18 inches in front of your head. Allow the hand to "slip" into the water. From this point, concentrate on the sensitivity of the water on your hand and forearm. You may go to full extension, or you may begin the high elbow underwater before you get to full extension. This will be a function of your personal style and strength.

Do this drill every day that you swim, 10 × 25 yards (meters)—or more if you are someone who has overreached for years.

was the windmill stroke of Janet Evans. Evans is arguably the best distance swimmer in history, and she had an extremely unorthodox stroke above the water in which she windmilled with a straight arm. The key is that her straight-arm recovery and entry did not affect her ability to get a hold of the water. She was able to find a sensitivity quickly upon entering, and then apply it to the high-elbow position under the water immediately. If you are able to do this too, then it is perfectly acceptable.

3. Catch-Up

Most of us know this drill. It is the one where we essentially swim normal freestyle except that the hand out front is waiting for the other hand to recover over the water and touch it before starting the pull. I almost did not include this drill, because it leads many people to think that the top swimmers do some sort of catch-up with their strokes and that this drill, with its emphasis on waiting out front, is training a glide-and-wait phase. This type of thinking could not be more off the mark.

Top swimmers do not glide. In fact, the phrase "front-quadrant swimming" has been fully misinterpreted by the masses as gliding out front. The hand that is out front, ready to pull, is not waiting for the other hand to come around. The true swimmer is working with tremendous sensitivity and strength to feel for the purchase of the water and begin the high-elbow position. At the same time, the core muscles, including the internal and external obliques, the transverse abdominal muscles, the lats, and the muscles surrounding the scapula, are engaging and loading the correct amount of tone/tension to drive the core forward. This is the most dynamic, important part of the swim stroke, thus the last thing a swimmer should do at this stage is be engaged in such a passive activity as gliding.

Look at the photo of Peter Vanderkaay (Figure 6.14). His right hand has just entered the water, and the pulling arm (left arm) is already significantly into the propulsive phase of the stroke. It makes no sense for Vanderkaay to glide with one hand out front while the other is recovering. If you do so, then which hand is providing forward propulsion? Neither. By gliding, not only is momentum lost, but also the rate of turnover slows dramatically, having an overall negative effect on our equation from Chapter 2.

FIGURE 6.14

PETER HAS ONE OF THE LONGEST STROKE RATES AMONG OLYMPIC SWIMMERS (1.6 SECONDS PER FULL STROKE CYCLE), YET EVEN WITH HIS LONG STROKE HIS PULLING HAND NEVER REMAINED EXTENDED—GLIDING—WAITING FOR THE RECOVERING ARM TO ENTER THE WATER.

This drill can be incorporated into a warm-up set to kick-start the workout into a focus on high elbow and feel, or it makes a great short set in the middle of a workout when fatigue is setting in and technique starts to fall apart. When a swimmer fatigues at practice, this drill is a great reminder to keep the high elbow and feel as the primary focus.

Whether you choose to incorporate the catch-up drill at the beginning or middle of your practice, do approximately 6–8 × 50 with 10–20 seconds of rest after each 50.

The truth behind front-quadrant swimming is that both hands are indeed in the front quadrant of the stroke length. They are both in front of, or near, the head, but the pulling hand/forearm has already done a huge amount of work to grab the water and get into the high-elbow position so that the body has driven forward to the point that it is about to pass over the pulling hand. All of this has taken place before the entry hand has even come close to extending. The pulling hand/forearm *never* stays in a glide position waiting for the other hand.

The concept of "extension" has been misconstrued as "gliding," and I believe the lack of understanding of core drive is the culprit. The reality of the underwater scene is that a truly effective core drive accentuates an acceleration of the finishing hand while providing natural extension to the hand that is initiating the catch. Top swimmers never remain static on the rotated side, gliding. Once the hips finish the drive to one side, the swimmer immediately switches direction to accentuate the drive to the other side. The drive and change of direction are only possible when the pulling hand has traction on the water and when the core muscles have been loaded with the correct amount of tension and tone.

The catch-up drill offers the swimmer time to pause and concentrate on the underwater pull, feel, and core drive, one arm at a time. When the finishing hand has recovered and touched the other hand, the primary focus is then placed on establishing the high-elbow position with the pulling arm (see Figure 6.15). Attention

FIGURE 6.15

ALLISON DEMONSTRATES THE CATCH-UP DRILL.

may also be placed on the feel for the water and application of pressure with the full paddle (forearm and hand working to apply pressure on the water as one unit, from the catch through to the finish of the stroke) as the swimmer drives his/her body forward in the water.

During the catch-up drill you will, to some degree, experience the feeling of lost momentum. Since there are phases when neither hand is propelling, we lose some momentum on each pull. It will never feel as completely fluid as when we actually swim the normal stroke with a rhythmic tempo. Do not rush the learning process, though. It takes time to develop a high elbow and feel before we can build tempo into the equation.

4. One Arm

Just as in the catch-up drill, the purpose of this drill is to concentrate on one arm at a time so that you may work the high elbow and feel without worrying about the timing of the full stroke. You may do this drill with the nonpulling arm at your side (as demonstrated in Figure 6.16) or out in front of you.

ONE-ARM DRILL

Do a full 25 yards (meters) with one arm, and then switch arms on the next length. Just as with the catch-up drill, you should expect a feeling of lost momentum. The important thing to remember is that this is to be done slowly, with concentration and sensitivity for feel. Always keep in mind that the second lever (the forearm and hand, which form the paddle), work as one unit to impulse on the water throughout the length of the underwater pull, from the catch to the finish.

At swim practice, incorporate this one-arm drill into your warm-up or include 6 × 50 as a low-intensity technique-based set, taking 10–20 seconds of rest after each 50. Stroke with the right arm for the first 25 yards (meters) and the left arm for the second 25.

FIGURE 6.17

ALLISON SHOWS PROPER TECHNIQUE FOR THE ONE-ARM PULL WITH KICKBOARD DRILL.

5. One-Arm Pull with Kickboard

I first saw this drill taught in 1999. Even though I was 30 years old and had been swimming for 25 years, this drill immediately became my favorite. In addition to developing a feel for the water, it builds strength everywhere.

The real benefits of this drill start to show when you are able to build in the feel for the water and core drive while you stroke. You will know if you are doing it correctly if the kickboard surges on each pull. Try to see how much of a surge you can build into the stroke as you engage in the high-elbow position (first third of the underwater pull) and throughout all three phases of the underwater pull, feeling an intuitive pressure on the water with your hand and forearm while driving the core forward. Remember to transition from the catch to the diagonal phase. Do not hold the high-elbow catch throughout the length of the pull. The correct aspects of the diagonal phase (the middle third) of the pull are that your upper arm navigates into a 45-degree downward angle, the elbow pointing away from the body. Your shoulders will build stability strength on this drill, too, because the arm that is placed on the kickboard does a fair amount of work to stabilize the body.

Place one hand in the middle of a kickboard. With your head above water and your legs kicking moderately, stroke with your free hand. The focus is placed first and foremost on the high-elbow position underwater. Watch your fingertips as your hand enters the water. Once you have reached extension with your arm, are your fingers pointing down as you begin to catch the water? Are they pointing down with a straight, flush wrist? Is your upper arm in front of you and seated high in the water (1–4 inches below the surface)? The answers to all of these questions should be "yes." See Figure 6.17 for an example of how to execute this drill properly.

Do 25 yards (meters) stroking with one arm; rest at the wall for approximately 15 seconds (you will be tired); then switch arms for the next 25. Do 12 × 25 total (6 × 25 each arm) three days per week.

BALANCING DRILLS WITH REGULAR SWIMMING

These exercises, focusing on high-elbow development and the feel, will keep you busy. Choose which work best for you. I still do them to this day for strength, range of motion, and the enjoyment of feeling the water, even though I have retired from competition. If I were still training and competing, I would certainly incorporate these exercises and drills into my workouts.

While drills are extremely beneficial for developing one or two aspects of the stroke at a time, you will go nuts if you train only drills for the next three months. I recommend including regular freestyle swimming (and other strokes, kicking, pulling, etc.) not only to keep your sanity, but also for a balanced training effect. Drills, drills, nothing but drills, will make you one of the most uncoordinated people on the planet. You will forget what you set out to do in the first place. Just remember that when you swim, *think* during every lap. Do not "check out" mentally and revert to old muscle memory. Constantly focus on developing your new muscle memory.

Keep in mind that while swimming it is impossible to think of every element of technique at one time, so focus on different aspects of the stroke at different times during the workout. Focus on your high-elbow catch; even take a peek at it now and then. Look to see that your fingertips are pointing toward the bottom of the pool during the early phase of the underwater pull; also look to see that the wrist is straight and flush during this phase. Then switch your attention to a sensitivity of feel, pressure, resistive forces, and traction—thinking about every point on your palm, wrist, forearm, and even the space between your fingers.

At times think about the spacing between your fingers. If the fingers are held properly (together but not tightly), with a slight spacing between, then there is a webbing-like effect, which increases the surface area of your hand for holding more water. Think about the muscles surrounding your scapula as you extend your arm to get into position for the high-elbow catch. Take note if your shoulder medially rotates toward your chin area as you catch the water. Push yourself to gain that flexibility even while you are swimming normally.

It will feel awkward, mechanical, and uncomfortable at first, but it is worth the journey. Soon enough you will be flowing into the position as if your body were originally designed for this range of motion.

A word of warning: Some of you will want to see a 5-second drop in your times on day one. Well, I am going to call you out on this. You are so focused on the product (your desired end result) that you have no time for considering the process (the elements that will actually take you to your desired end result). Remember our discussion in Chapter 3 about being a craftsperson? Slow down and switch your mode of thinking to one that is more process-oriented. This is called "the journey," and it is the loveliest part of sport.

Performance results are fleeting anyway. I have an Olympic gold medal in my closet, yet today I will clean the kitty litter twice, do the dishes, throw in a load of laundry, and go to the mailbox, where I will be greeted by a stack of bills just like all of you will. But . . . today, if I choose, I may go to the pool, dive in, and feel the water. I may engage my mind in activities to take my body a fraction closer to its full future potential. That is a great day in sport, and in life.

FINDING YOUR FOCUS

When you feel fatigue in practice, especially during the all-out swims, this is the most important time to maintain a high elbow and traction on the water. Do not allow your elbow to drop due to fatigue. Stay composed; focus on technique. Not only does this do wonders for your physical strength and muscle memory (because this is when the "training effect" sets in), but also it is what puts the meaning back into the mental side of sport. It is called mental toughness and focus.

Focus means thinking about the things that are within your control. Technique is always in your control.

Learn how to focus regularly in practice. Your times may just drop to levels you never knew you had in you.

1. **The vital elements** of a propulsive pull, the high elbow, and feel for the water may be trained in a variety of in-water and out-of-water exercises.

2. **Tissue does respond.** Although some of the exercises and drills can be tiring and difficult at first, a swimmer who concentrates on them at each practice will see gains in strength, flexibility, and feel within weeks.

3. Even if you are new to focusing on the vital elements of a propulsive pull, be sure to incorporate **freestyle swimming** into your workouts rather than just the drills.

4. **When fatigue sets in** during practice, that is the most important time to regain control of technique. A mini drill set of 6 × 25 or 6 × 50, focusing on the critical elements of a strong pull, will get a swimmer back on track.

5. Remember: ***Fatigue is an opportunity to become stronger.***

THE SWIMMING EQUATION APPLIED
STROKE COUNTS & RATES OF TOP SWIMMERS

Chapter 6 focused on learning the technique of the underwater pull, and it stressed the need to slow down and concentrate while developing new muscle memory. This is extremely important; swimming is first and foremost about technique. Without technique, strength and conditioning mean little. Eventually, however, if we want to be fast, power and speed must be built into the stroke.

The swimming equation (Number of Strokes) × (Rate of Turnover) = Time is our guiding star. In Chapter 2, I offered two examples of this equation in action. To refresh your memory, we singled out the "long glider" whose turnover rate was disastrously slow, and then we looked at the enthusiastic 8-and-under swimmers who spun their arms wildly and took a record-breaking number of strokes to get across the pool.

The numbers I plugged into those equations were simply examples. In this chapter we will look at the real numbers. Most important, I want to tie what we have learned about propulsion and the underwater pull together with our guiding-star equation.

First, however, two factors in the equation must be reviewed: Number of strokes and rate of turnover. The underwater pull affects both dramatically. Let's jump right in and look at the real numbers.

PLUGGING IN THE NUMBERS

The stroke rates of top swimmers are consistently in the range of 1.15 seconds per full stroke cycle to 1.6 seconds per full stroke cycle. Sprinters (50-m and 100-m specialists) typically have a faster rate, sometimes even under 1 second per full cycle, but usually between 1.0 and 1.2 seconds.

Do these numbers sound quick? They should, because they are. You might be asking yourself, "Does this mean that even the big guys are only taking one and a half seconds per full arm cycle through the water? It looks so much longer and slower than that." Well, it is indeed just as you have guessed. Even the swimmers who extend the most (Ian Thorpe of Australia, Michael Phelps, and many other top men) have rates of only 1.5–1.6 seconds per full arm cycle.

These stroke-rate numbers prove that top swimmers do not glide. There simply is no time for their arms to remain out in front, gliding twice (remember, each arm is part of one full cycle), and still make it around in 1.5 seconds. And we are talking about the *longest* stroke rates right now. The most common rates are even faster—1.3 to 1.4 seconds per cycle.

So, just what is it they are doing? You already know the answer. They are getting into the high-elbow position so as to be able to hold the water and do what a real swimmer does: drive the body over the hand and arm that have just "purchased"

Remember: When we talk about rate of turnover, we are counting full stroke cycles (from the time the right arm enters the water until it enters again, or left arm to left arm).

FIGURE 7.1

PETER DISPLAYS THE HIGH-ELBOW POSITION THAT IS CRITICAL FOR OPTIMIZING THE STROKE COUNT AND RATE EQUATION.

the water (see Figure 7.1). This is how elite swimmers get distance per stroke. Even the swimmers who fully extend their arms are feeling the sensitivity of the water the entire time so that they may get into their high-elbow position and continue the momentum of the stroke immediately after extension.

Once the swimmer is in a high-elbow position, then the path the hand takes does not sweep wide and far to find still water. It is predominantly a backward path (remember, we need to move forward) with impulses (sculls) and diagonal angles to find still water.

Just as a long glide out front kills our turnover rate, so too does a long and meandering path under the water. Your pull pattern must find still water in order to maintain resistance that moves you forward, but you need not launch a full-fledged search expedition to find it.

Spend time looking closely at the photos in this book. You will learn more from studying those than from anything I could write in words.

OPTIMIZING THE EQUATION

Putting sprinters aside for a moment, why do some top middle-distance and distance swimmers (200-m to 1500-m swimmers) have a 1.1-second rate and others a 1.6-second rate?

As mentioned at the beginning of Chapter 5, some top swimmers get into the high-elbow position almost immediately when their hand enters the water. Their strokes appear choppy and short, almost crab-like. They do not extend to a full straight arm. These swimmers' rates are often in the range of 1.15 to 1.2 seconds. They will take more strokes than other swimmers, but their rates are considerably quicker. They are optimizing the two numbers in the equation in a manner that best suits their strength, flexibility, and personal attributes.

These quick 1.15- to 1.2-second turnovers and shorter stroke lengths, when seen in top swimmers, are most commonly seen in female distance swimmers. While the equation for these swimmers is optimized in many ways, the shortcoming is that such a stroke does not support the really high gears of swimming speed. When they are entered in a shorter event that requires more speed (the 50-m and 100-m), many of them find it difficult to effectively employ a more powerful stroke. This does not matter so much, however, since their forte is distance swimming (400-m and above).

This example is not meant to imply that all female distance swimmers stroke with quick turnovers and shorter pulls. The intent of the example is to show that it is one option for balancing the equation. It works for a certain percentage of top swimmers. I do believe, however, that women's distance swimming is shifting away from this, as strength training is increasingly a part of every swimmer's program now. Distance swimming is not solely about tempo and aerobic fitness any longer; strength and power are coming into the equation. The stroke-rate and stroke-count numbers included at the end of this chapter show this trend.

To have the most power output, a swimmer must have the capability of turning over quickly while holding the water effectively. Sprinters offer the perfect example of optimizing the equation in this way. They employ a powerful stroke, holding onto the water while employing the fastest turnovers seen in elite swimming (under 1.0 to 1.05 seconds for 50-m swimmers and 1.05 to 1.2 seconds for 100-m swimmers). The limitation here is in maintaining power and speed over a longer distance; therefore, just as a distance swimmer has difficulty switching to a more powerful gear, many sprinters are at a loss to find a gear that works for longer races.

Both groups have a feel for the water and high-elbow catch (except sprinters who train the straight-arm technique; see Appendix B). It is the manner in which they apply force and speed to the stroke that determines whether they are more suited for being distance specialists or sprinters.

Middle-distance swimmers also rely on the vital elements of a high elbow and feel while optimizing the balance of stroke count and stroke rate for their event. Since some middle-distance swimmers are sprint oriented while others are distance oriented, the range of numbers in stroke rate and stroke count among this group varies. Some will tend toward a longer, more powerful stroke with a slower turnover (1.5–1.6 seconds), while others swim with a shorter stroke length and faster turnover (1.2–1.4 seconds).

The most strategic middle-distance race is the 200. Not only will you see a wide range of turnover rates among swimmers in a pool, but also you will see a single swimmer changing his or her rate within the 200. A 200 swimmer will often employ a 1.4- to 1.6-second rate during the first 100 of a 200, and then will pick up the tempo on the last 100, or the last 50, and stroke at a rate one-tenth of a second faster or more per full stroke cycle. This is part of a strategy that the swimmer and coach design to maximize the equation at various points of such a strategic race.

The bottom line is that there are no rules. The general range is 1.0–1.6 seconds, and this covers just about every top swimmer in the spectrum. The top athletes are optimizing the equation in a way that best suits them and their event. The key is that they are aware that the equation needs to be optimized.

Unfortunately, I see many swimmers still focused on one thing: reducing resistance through body position, gliding, and overreaching. The rates of triathletes and masters swimmers are almost always over 2.0 seconds per full stroke cycle, and they go as high as 3.0. You will see in this chapter that even the longest Olympic stroke rates (1.5–1.6) are significantly faster than the rates of swimmers who focus on gliding.

High-elbow position and feel are key to increasing distance per stroke (taking fewer strokes) while not sacrificing rate of turnover. Athletes who glide out front may be able to take as few strokes as the top swimmers, but they are virtually twice as slow due to rate of turnover.

WHAT'S YOUR EQUATION?

In order to determine your own equation, you need to know your own stroke rate and stroke count.

Since it is impossible for you to swim and operate a stopwatch at the same time, you will have to ask someone to take your rate for you. It does not matter which arm they time. The key is that they start the watch when your arm enters the water, and then stop it when that same arm has completed a full cycle and enters the water again. They should take it multiple times throughout a 100-yard (or 100-m) swim. They should also occasionally time two full cycles and then divide the number in half. This minimizes minor errors in their timing. Ask whoever is timing your rate to do so when you are swimming at race tempo, rather than at a slower warm-up or warm-down tempo. The numbers presented on elite swimmers in this chapter are taken from race efforts. An elite swimmer's tempo during

Remember: When counting, be sure to include the first half-stroke, which takes place under the water before your breakout.

easy-to-moderate swimming at practice is approximately two-tenths of a second to 1 second slower than their race pace tempo.

Counting strokes is not difficult, but it does require concentration. You can count your own strokes, but it is not a bad idea to have a coach or friend count them for you as well. It does not matter if you are in a 25-yard pool, a 25-m pool, or a 50-m pool for counting, but you will only be able to make comparisons between your stroke count and the stroke counts of others if you are comparing from pools of the same length. Every stroke count I took for this chapter was taken from Olympic swimming races (50-m pool); thus for you to make comparisons with those counts, you must be measured in a 50-m pool.

WHICH TO TRAIN FIRST, TECHNIQUE OR TEMPO?

Some of you may now have a fire in your belly to get to the pool immediately and start working on a 1.3–1.4 tempo. That might sound like a great idea, especially for the type A personalities in the group. Stop! Slow down. Do not go the route of the 8-and-under swimmer. Remember, that does not work any better than a long glide.

"Power and speed" are not the same as "hurrying and rushing." Olympic swimmers have developed the vital element of *feel*, from the moment of the high-elbow catch through the diagonal phase and finish of the stroke. Trust me when I say that the turnover speed can be developed later. You must first develop an entirely new muscle memory if you have never thought about a high elbow and feel before. This requires thoughtful concentration. Within a few months, if you have exercised patience, then you will be ready to start thinking about power, speed, and the rate side of the equation.

Interestingly, for those of you who have been gliding or doing an exaggerated S pull, your tempo will automatically speed up simply by taking a more efficient pull path through the water. It will feel strange and almost wrong, because the rhythm to which you were so accustomed is now going to change. Work with the new rhythm. It is not wrong; it is right. Do not bail out of making a beneficial change just because it "doesn't feel right." I am calling you out on this again like I did in Chapter 6. Do not be product oriented. Focus on the process.

1996 AND 2008 OLYMPIC
STROKE RATES AND STROKE COUNTS

This section presents a compilation of stroke rates and stroke counts of Olympic medalists in various freestyle events. The numbers were gathered as I played and replayed video from the 1996 Olympics in Atlanta and the 2008 Olympics in Beijing. I make no claim that the numbers are accurate to a hundreth of a second, but they are close enough so as to make relevant conclusions on certain matters.

Some of the information I present is more complete on certain swimmers than others. This is simply due to the television coverage. Often I was unable to count strokes on a field of swimmers when the TV camera panned in on the leader for any significant period of time. In those cases, I present as much information as was possible to gather.

Note that since these numbers are taken from Olympic swimming races, the pool length was 50 meters. If you are interested in comparing your stroke count to that of an Olympic swimmer, then you need to be in a 50-m pool. The counts are not the same if you swim in a 25-m pool and double the number, due to the turn at the wall.

Olympic Women

Note: The following numbers do not include the first 50 meters due to the distance generated by the starting dive.

★ 1996 Olympic gold medalist, 800-m freestyle, BROOKE BENNETT of the United States (8:27.89): Bennett on average took **26 to 26.5 stroke cycles** per 50 meters at a rate of approximately **1.15 seconds per cycle**.

★ 1996 Olympic silver medalist, 800-m freestyle, DAGMAR HASE of Germany (8:29.91): Hase on average took **24 stroke cycles** per 50 meters at a rate of approximately **1.25 seconds per cycle**.

★ 2008 Olympic gold medalist, 800-m freestyle, REBECCA ADLINGTON of Great Britain (8:14.10): Adlington on average took **20 stroke cycles** per 50 meters at a rate of **1.38–1.4 seconds per cycle**.

★ 2008 Olympics: the 800-m freestyle silver medalist, ALESSIA FILIPPI of Italy, stroked at a rate of **1.5–1.6**, and the bronze medalist, LOTTE FRIIS of Denmark, turned over at **1.35–1.4 seconds per cycle** (stroke counts not available due to television coverage).

★ 1996 Olympic gold medalist, 200-m freestyle, CLAUDIA POLL of Costa Rica (1:58.16): Poll on average took **25 stroke cycles** per 50 meters at a rate of approximately **1.13 seconds per cycle**.

★ 1996 Olympic silver medalist, 200-m freestyle, FRANZISKA VAN ALMSICK of Germany (1:58.57): Van Almsick on average took **20 stroke cycles** per 50 meters at a rate of approximately **1.4 seconds per cycle**.

★ 2008 Olympic gold medalist, 200-m freestyle, FEDERICA PELLEGRINI of Italy (1:54.82): Pellegrini on average took **21 to 21.5 stroke cycles** per 50 meters at a rate of approximately **1.25 seconds per cycle** (note that in the 400-m freestyle in Beijing, Pellegrini took 20.5 stroke cycles per 50 at a rate of 1.35 seconds per cycle).

★ 2008 Olympics, fourth place, 200-m freestyle, KATIE HOFF of the United States (1:55.78): Hoff on average took **20 to 20.5 stroke cycles** per 50 meters at a rate of approximately **1.3 seconds per cycle.**

★ The 2008 U.S. women's 4 × 200-m freestyle relay bronze medalists all stroked around **1.3 seconds per cycle.** The Australian gold medalists in the same relay stroked in the range of **1.2–1.4 seconds per cycle.**

★ 2008 Olympics: DARA TORRES of the United States, on the second 50 meters of the 100-m freestyle (on her leg of the 4 × 100 m freestyle relay), took **20 strokes** at a rate of **1.25 seconds per stroke.**

Olympic Men

★ 2008 Olympic gold medalist, 400-m freestyle, PARK TAE-HWAN of Korea (3:41.86): Park on average took **17 stroke cycles** per 50 meters at a rate of approximately **1.5 seconds per stroke.** (On the last 100 meters, Park stroked at a rate of 1.3.)

★ 2008 Olympic bronze medalist, 400-m freestyle, LARSEN JENSEN of the United States (3:42.78): Larsen on average took **17 stroke cycles** per 50 meters at a rate of approximately **1.55 seconds per cycle.** (On the last 100 meters, Larsen stroked at a rate of 1.3. His stroke count went to 19.5.)

★ 1996 Olympic gold medalist, 200-m freestyle, DANIEL LOADER of New Zealand (1:47.63): Loader on average took **19.5 stroke cycles** per 50 meters at a rate of approximately **1.3 seconds per stroke.**

★ 2008 Olympic gold medalist, 200-m freestyle, MICHAEL PHELPS of the United States (1:42.96): Phelps on average took **14.5 stroke cycles** per 50 meters at a rate of **1.5–1.55 seconds per stroke.**

★ 2008 Olympic silver medalist, 200-m freestyle, PARK TAE-HWAN
   of Korea (1:44.85): Park on average took **18 stroke cycles** per 50 meters
   at a rate of approximately **1.35 seconds per stroke**.

★ 1996 Olympic gold medal, 4 × 200-m freestyle relay team of the United States:
   The average number of stroke cycles per 50 meters among all four swimmers
   was **18 to 19**, and their stroke rates were consistently in the range of **1.35–1.4
   seconds per stroke**.

★ 2008 Olympic gold medalist, during his anchor leg of the 4 × 200-m freestyle relay, PETER VANDERKAAY of the United States (relay split 1:44.7):
   Vanderkaay on average took **16.5 stroke cycles** per 50 meters at a rate of
   approximately **1.55 seconds per stroke**.

   *It is interesting to note that Vanderkaay changed his stroke rate throughout the 200.
   Below is a recap of each 50 meters.*

   First 50: 14 strokes at 1.55 (consider the dive off the blocks when looking
   at stroke count)
   Second 50: 15 strokes at 1.55
   Third 50: 16.5 strokes at 1.4
   Fourth 50: 17.5 strokes at 1.35–1.38

★ 2008 Olympic gold medalist, 100-m freestyle, ALAIN BERNARD of France
   (47.21): Bernard took **20 stroke cycles** on his second 50 meters, at a rate of
   approximately **1.1 seconds per stroke**. (Bernard stayed underwater after the
   turn for approximately 2.5 seconds.)

★ 2008 Olympic bronze medalist, 100-m freestyle, JASON LEZAK of the
   United States (47.67): Lezak took **18 stroke cycles** on his second 50 meters at
   a rate of **1.25–1.3 seconds per stroke**. (Jason stayed underwater after the
   turn for approximately 3.1 seconds.)

FIGURE 7.2

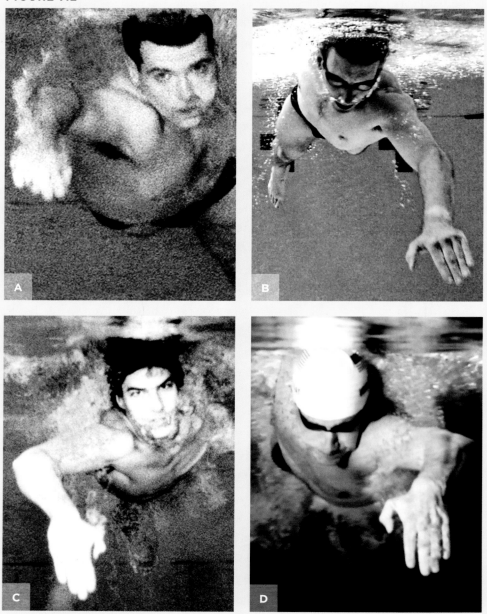

THREE OF THESE HOLDS ARE CORRECT; ONE IS NOT. CAN YOU TELL WHICH ONE IS NOT CORRECT?

Please note that the number of stroke cycles per 50 meters is, in part, affected by how long a swimmer stays underwater kicking off the turns. International rules allow for a maximum of 15 meters. Most swimmers do not stay under for the full 15 meters, but some stay under longer than others. Michael Phelps, for instance, kicked underwater for more than 4 seconds, while silver medalist Park Tae-Hwan of Korea was underwater for approximately 2.5 seconds after the turns. The length of time underwater obviously affects the stroke count.

Also note, when measuring stroke rates, the variations in time from stroke to stroke, even within one 50-m length, can vary slightly due to a number of factors (i.e., the swimmer taking a breath, fatigue setting in, and natural variations that come from humans not being machines). For triathletes, the variations in rate can be even greater due to open-water conditions. Interestingly, at the 1996 Olympics I stroked at a rate of 1.25 in the 200-m freestyle in the pool; whereas, at the 2000 Olympics in triathlon (open-water swimming), my rate was in the range of 1.3–1.5 depending on the waves and water conditions.

So now, a test. Figure 7.2 contains photographs of four underwater holds. Three are correct; one is incorrect. Can you tell which is the incorrect underwater arm position?

The perpetrator of the "low elbow" in photograph B is a dear friend of mine named Jim. He is 37 years old, strong, fit, a fantastic marathon runner (2:56:58) and triathlete, and as you can see in Figure 7.3, he has great body position, head position, and timing. He averages 1:29 per 100 yards when doing a 30-minute swim at best effort, which is good for someone who did not grow up swimming. He has the potential, however, to be 15 seconds faster per 100 yards by taking the same amount of time he now spends in the water (three days per week on good weeks) and focusing solely on the high-elbow position and feel.

The number of strokes Jim takes to get across the pool is the same as what I take, but his rate of turnover is 1.9 seconds per full stroke cycle swimming at his triathlon race pace. He attempts to get a fairly long reach or extension during the front phase of his stroke and then pushes downward with his hand to get to a depth to pull back under his body. His arm and elbow stay straight during the early phase of the stroke (no high elbow). My rate of turnover at the same effort is 1.3. I am

FIGURE 7.3

JIM HAS AN IDEAL BODY POSITION, HEAD POSITION, HIP ROTATION, AND TIMING.
THE ONLY THING MISSING IS THE HIGH ELBOW, WHICH IS THE KEY TO PROPULSION AND
RATE OF TURNOVER.

not trying any harder to get that faster turnover; instead I am getting into the high-elbow position early in the stroke so as to hold the water in a way that will move me forward. I have no glide out front (though I do dynamically extend and drive my core muscles), nor is my hand taking a long path under the water. My hand/forearm takes a predominantly backward path below me, with intuitive impulses that maintain the resistive friction and feel for the water.

If the six-tenths of a second per stroke cycle difference is multiplied by the number of strokes taken for a 100-yard freestyle (approximately 8 full strokes per

25 yards), then I will be 4.8 seconds faster per 25 yards (8 strokes × 0.6 rate = 4.8). That will translate into 19.2 seconds per 100 yards. I will also gain time on him during the streamlines off the wall (another 0.5 to 1 second per turn most likely), because he does not work each streamline 100 percent in practice, having never fully considered the benefits and importance of it.

By the way, are you wondering how you ask a friend if they are willing to be the subject of how *not* to do something in your book? There were about 100 people I could have called who have the same low elbow. The only one who I knew would not take it personally was Jim, because he has a great sense of humor and a humble spirit. Plus, I promised him that I would inform readers that he could beat me in any distance running race and any bike sprint for a city-limit sign.

1. **Number of Strokes × Rate = Time.**

2. The **fastest swimmers in the world** turn over at a rate of 1.0–1.6 seconds per full stroke cycle.

3. Swimmers who attempt to **reduce their stroke count by gliding out front** have rates of turnover between 2.0–3.0 seconds per full stroke cycle.

4. **Top swimmers are able to reduce their stroke count** without increasing their rate of turnover because they catch the water in a high-elbow position and drive their bodies over their pulling hand/arm. Their rate of turnover is fast because their hand/arm did not passively glide out front or take a long, meandering S-pull path under the water.

PIECING IT ALL TOGETHER

CONCLUSIONS & "CALLING THE SUIT"

We are at the end of the book, and I am worried about one thing. I am worried that I made my point so well about the pull being the vital factor that you are all like Frankenstein's monster now. I am a little nervous that you are going to show up to practice and cause havoc at your swim team or triathlon group, insisting that Pareto be honored. It's either that, or I am going to be at a triathlon or swim meet one day and see you swimming like Tarzan. Don't do that, please.

(Actually, if you win the 100 freestyle at your next swim meet or lead out of T-1 at your next triathlon swimming like Johnny Weissmuller, then I am going to be the first to shake your hand.)

Seriously though, remember to keep everything in context. Yes, the pull is the vital factor. Without it you are never going to be a really fast swimmer; however, a number of other components to stroke technique must be addressed as well. The other 80 percent does impact performance, so those elements deserve a percentage of our attention, especially once the pull is well developed. None will get the leading role the pull gets, but the others are either supporting actors or part of the behind-the-scenes crew.

Our supporting actors are elements such as the kick and using the body core to accentuate power. These do not make for a good story on their own, but at the same time, the real character of the pull is not fully revealed without them.

The behind-the-scenes crew includes elements of the stroke such as knowing how to breathe and establishing a body position on top of the water. Without these, the door to the theater would never be unlocked. Their importance should not be minimized, especially for beginners, but I encourage a mindset that recognizes we need to move past these at the moment we have established a comfort with the water.

I've addressed some of the nonvital elements in Appendix B ("Ask an Olympian"). I address these elements only so far as to show how they tie in with the underwater pull, because the basics are thoroughly explained on dozens of websites and in every swim-technique book at the bookstore. I see no reason to rewrite what is already available.

My mission in this book is to fill the gaping hole that has existed since humans first took to competitive swimming. This book was born out of recognition that someone had to sort the overwhelming amount of information for you. More than that, the intent was to introduce the thinking tools that will guide you to sort information for yourself. The tools apply to any area of your life that involves productivity goals.

WHAT 80/20 LOOKS LIKE IN PRACTICE

Here is an example of how, during a workout, I apply a portion of my 20 percent focus on the 80 percent of nonvital aspects of freestyle technique. Since many people overemphasize body-position considerations in practice, I chose to demonstrate four situations in training in which body position is my focus.

As a "check." Sporadically in the middle of a swim set I check my position. Especially if I am fatiguing toward the end of a workout, I turn my attention to whether or not my body position is dropping in the water and my head is steady. The "check" takes only a fraction of a second. Our body position is much less dynamic than our pulling arms, so once we establish the position we want, we need only minimal concentration to hold it there.

As a tool to ensure my stroke has power. I turn my attention to my core in order to drive power into my stroke, if the swim set is meant to be done with speed and power. This has more to do with getting a desired training effect than with technique. In these instances, I primarily work the high-elbow aspect of the pull, but I am also cognizant of holding a strong tone in my core and driving more powerfully and at a quicker tempo. The core, including the hips, must keep pace with arm turnover; if you engage the high-elbow catch more quickly during a sprint, then the core drive must become more dynamic as well.

As a stroke technique drill. I most often choose drills that involve a high elbow and feel for the water, but every once in a while I will work on a different aspect of the stroke, such as the hips finishing the core drive rhythmically. Whereas many people think about hip roll as a method of reducing resistance, I encourage swimmers to think of it primarily in terms of rhythmically accentuating the pull.

On the tow machine. The tow machine is a unique tool that is not readily available to most people. A swimmer wears a belt around the waist, and a cable is attached from the belt to a pulley system above the water. The pulley system can be set to any speed the swimmer or coach chooses, even faster than the men's 50-m freestyle world record. The swimmer may either hold a streamline position as he or she is pulled the length of the pool, or the swimmer may try to stroke at a rate fast enough to keep up with the machine. There is no tool in swimming that shines a light more brightly on the theoretical square law (resistance increases exponentially as velocity increases), so testing and tweaking head and body position produce fascinating results.

Contrast this occasional focus on body position with the amount of concentration placed on the pull. From the moment I dive in the water for warm-up, I think about a high-elbow position and feel for the water. These remain at the forefront of concentration throughout the entire workout. Even if the position becomes natural for a swimmer, the range of motion of the position still needs to be worked along with the strength that goes into holding the water. *Feel* for the water is not only the most important part of the stroke, but it is also the most enjoyable. How fortunate that our sport affords us the gift of enjoying what is most important for success.

TAKING A PLAN TO THE POOL

The following sections of this chapter include my advice to the three types of readers I suspect have picked up this book: experienced swimmers who want to reach the next level; swimmers and triathletes who have focused on body position and gliding for years, with frustrating results; and adults learning to swim.

EXPERIENCED SWIMMERS WHO WANT TO REACH THE NEXT LEVEL

If you are an experienced swimmer, even at the collegiate level, you should be concentrating the majority of your technique focus on feel, hold, and the high elbow during aerobic sets, endurance sets, anaerobic sets, sprinting, warm-up/warm-down, and every other set. The position can always be developed for more range and strength, even if you think you are doing it quite well already. I wish I had known, back in my high school and college days, how to do that. All the lengths up and down the pool, when I was alone with my thoughts, could have been better applied to something useful instead of thinking about being hungry, that the water was cold, or how I could not wait until the 2-hour practice was over.

Swim with focus. Make each practice count. Know why you do what you do, every day. If you have a rough day, do not be hard on yourself; make something of it. Even if you are fatigued to the point of not making the intervals, then think about streamlining, holding the water, or gaining range of motion in the high-elbow position. You should leave every practice able to verbalize, "I just became better today, because. . . ."

Your greatest gains will come when you work the high elbow and hold during anaerobic or lactate sets (all-out swims). Many athletes spend energy trying to think of ways to avoid the pain during these sets when they should be focusing on strengthening the underwater pull (and the kick for those who are six-beat kickers). (See Appendix B for information on the kick.)

Also, meet with your coach to discuss stroke tempo. Analyze your rate compared to the rates of Olympic medalists (Chapter 7). You are in charge of figuring out how to optimize the two factors of the swimming equation. It is all logic and common sense, around which a specific plan may be built. Start building that plan today.

SWIMMERS AND TRIATHLETES WHO HAVE FOCUSED ON BODY POSITION AND GLIDING FOR YEARS, WITH FRUSTRATING RESULTS

If you fall into this category, then your mindset must be flipped on its head. Simply stated, within this group, a revolution needs to take place. In order to move quickly through the water, you are going to have to design a plan that works the underwater pull the majority of the time—80 percent of the time, in fact. Throw your obsession with gliding, streamlining, and reducing resistance right out the window. It is making you slow. Trade it in for increasing resistance on the water underneath you for the sake of traction.

The information in Chapter 7 on stroke rates and stroke counts of Olympic swimmers has always been available. I am baffled at how it has not been the center of every swimming-technique discussion. If it had been, then I believe the past 15 years would have proved more productive for swimmers and triathletes who have been wondering what they were missing.

What was missing was the full story. Believe it or not, that is good news. You now have the information that should infuse your workouts with a new round of enthusiasm. Be sure to focus on technique before building the rate side of the equation. You have plenty of time. Do not rush the process. Those of you who understand that a strong underwater pull takes time are going to succeed at swimming; whereas, those who rush the process will remain frustrated.

ADULTS LEARNING TO SWIM

As mentioned, some aspects of the freestyle swim stroke, such as comfort in the water and breathing technique, are necessary for beginners to learn before anything else. Those will be your vital elements for a short while. There is absolutely no reason though why a beginner cannot do dry-land exercises (tubing, Halo bench, and press-outs) and a few in-water drills (sculling, even if simply standing like Gary Hall Jr. did) to develop feel and a high elbow.

Coaches who work with adults learning to swim should have compassion for the challenges of establishing a comfort level in the water, but they should also not underestimate their swimmer's ability to handle the most advanced elements of the swim stroke. Even if a woman approached me and said that she was 70 years old, had never done an athletic event in her life, but wanted to learn to swim in order to compete in a triathlon, I would introduce her to tubing and sculling on the first day.

Every person, no matter his or her age, level of experience, or level of strength and flexibility, is capable of making progress toward the vital elements of swimming.

Note: For those of you who are not yet comfortable with the water, please review the section on sculling regularly. Take note of the way the hands are held—with tone, not cupped. Place your focus on *feeling* the pressure of the water on your forearms and hands, and you will begin to have a calm control over your body in the water. Panic comes when we fight the water and become rigid, so slow down and focus on the feel. If you do this, then you will see the sport from an entirely new perspective, and your comfort level will improve dramatically.

ONE MORE GROUP

Some of you, after reading everything that is involved with going fast, will choose a long, gliding, less-taxing swim stroke for your style. You may not be concerned with speed and winning. You may just want to enjoy the sport for all of its other benefits. Beautiful. I admire you for calling the suit, and I would be your euchre partner anytime.

SORTING THROUGH IT ALL: KNOWING WHAT TO WORK ON AND WHEN

We know that strength and conditioning provide little benefit unless a swimmer is holding the water, so the technique for an effective underwater pull must be developed before anything else. Once the technique is established, training becomes more critical. Methodologies in training and conditioning are as numerous as technique elements of the swim stroke, so again we are faced with sorting through massive amounts of information in order to identify which elements are vital.

A young athlete may need to build an aerobic base, whereas an experienced, older swimmer with a well-established aerobic base may identify that speed is the critical factor. Swimmers and coaches should look at the big picture and determine which aspects of training are most crucial.

Multisport athletes have to manage the big picture even more than single-sport athletes. Knowing when to back off training one discipline in order to have energy for training another discipline is challenging. Applying the reasoning that underlies the 80/20 rule is useful in sorting through the choices, as is the law of diminishing returns.

Also, be sure to reevaluate your situation on a regular basis. You are never the same athlete from season to season. Hopefully, you have developed new strengths over the course of a year. Know yourself and the cards you are dealt, and then make confident decisions from there.

GETTING EUCHRED

To wrap things up, do you see why those in the elite swimming world are breaking records left and right? They are optimizing the equation from Chapter 2. They are taking fewer strokes at a faster rate and accomplishing it via an amazing hold on the water below. Their focus is in the deep blue third dimension.

Elite swimmers are by nature hard workers, but you must recognize that their strength training and conditioning are only meaningful because of the hold. The masses of swimmers and triathletes who train diligently day after day and see no improvement in their times are failing because they have nothing solid upon which to place the hard work. We can correct this, thank goodness.

You may not have a six-figure sponsorship, nor access to the top training equipment that some elite athletes have, but you have access to the same water. Water does not discriminate. It is there for the taking. So, do what Johnny Weissmuller did, and get a purchase on the elusive.

This is your life! You may get euchred if you take a risk, but at least you boldly played the game. What does "getting euchred" mean? In cards, it means that you called the trump suit, but your competition was dealt a better hand and beat you. It happens occasionally in life, too. I got euchred during the fencing portion of the pentathlon in Beijing. It was still worth it!

Call the suit!

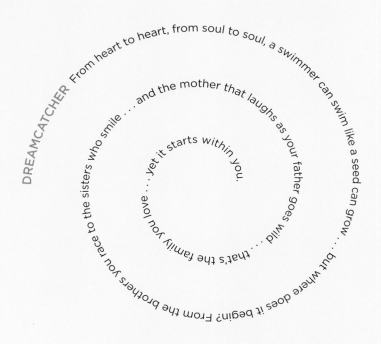

DREAMCATCHER From heart to heart, from soul to soul, a swimmer can swim like a seed can grow . . . but where does it begin? From the brothers you race to the sisters who smile . . . and the mother that laughs as your father goes wild . . . that's the family you love . . . yet it starts within you.

*A poem from my nieces and nephews
before the 1996 Olympics*

TAORMINA'S TOP 20
CHANGES IN SWIMMING SINCE 1924

Below is a Top 20 list of everything I could think of, or was led to discover during the research for this book, that appears to have been a contributing factor in the improvement of swimming times since Weissmuller's day. It includes discoveries in technique, improvements in training methods, and new inventions. I made this list for two reasons:

- For fun. There is some great historical perspective in the list.
- To toast Pareto one last time, because the 80/20 notation he made more than 100 years ago stands true with regard to swimming technique and performance impact. If you take Weissmuller's 57.4-second world record and compare it with the current world record set by Cesar Cielo of 46.9 seconds, there is a 20 percent differential. That proves that a powerful pull, which is the only common denominator between Weissmuller and Cielo, other than the fact that they both competed in water, is 80 percent of competitive swimming. Everything else on this list adds up to the other 20 percent.

TOP 20 LIST OF CHANGES AND DEVELOPMENTS
IN SWIMMING SINCE 1924

1. **Starting blocks.** First used in 1936. Before that, swimmers dove off the side of the pool.

2. **Flip turns.** First came onto the scene in the 1950s.

3. **Shaving down.** First thought of as a way to reduce resistance in the 1950s by the Australians.

4. **Wind-up starts.** Prior to the early 1970s, swimmers did not grab the starting blocks.

5. **Entry angle of dive.** Weissmuller describes his entry into the water, and he truly believed it was superior:

   My starting plunge is worthy of a little extended study. . . . My head is down and I am looking with open eyes at the water. . . . One leg is raised much higher than the other. These things do not just happen; every point here means something. When I hit the water, I bring my arms down with a powerful slap, and at the same time I bring my raised leg down with a tremendous plop. I look at the water so as to time this slap of the arms and leg exactly at the moment of my entry into the water. . . . Making the shallow plunge, keeping high in the water by slapping down with my arms and leg, I am ready to begin swimming sooner than my rivals. (Weissmuller 1930, 27)

   Also, remember the pike dive that was hugely popular into the 1970s? It did nothing more for swimmers than Weissmuller's starting plunge, since both stop the explosive power from the push off the blocks almost immediately upon entry.

6. **Invention of competitive swimming goggles.** First introduced in the early 1970s, goggles enhanced a swimmer's vision in the water. At the 1972 Olympics in Munich, goggles were not allowed. The first Olympics with goggles was in 1976.

7. **Longer training sessions.** In addition to enhancing a swimmer's vision, goggles also impacted training methods. Swimmers could stay in the water longer, thus longer training sessions were possible, positively affecting aerobic capacities and endurance capabilities in swimmers.

8. **Advancements in scientific research.** In recent decades, sports science, psychology, training research, physiology labs, zone training, heart-rate training, biomechanical analysis, and the study of fluid dynamics have been funded for research to improve training methods and overall performance.

9. **Nutrition and hydration.** The availability of high-quality organic and natural foods, protein drinks, recovery foods, and energy bars, and the education on the importance of hydration, did not come on the scene until the 1980s. My twin brother reminded me that we never used water bottles when we swam in high school in the mid-1980s.

10. **Body position and streamlining.** Weissmuller definitely thought he was onto something with his reasoning behind hydroplaning, but we have come a long way in truly understanding body-position considerations. We have also learned a great deal about using the body core to accentuate the power that is generated from holding the water with the limbs.

11. **Strength training and core power training.** The focus on strength and core power today is significant compared to the 1980s and even the 1990s. You will be hard-pressed to find any top collegiate swim program that does not have access to a state-of-the-art strength facility and specialized strength coaches.

12. **Inventions.** Power racks, power tower, the Halo bench, towing machines, monofins, in-water parachutes, and a number of other strength and power tools provide training options that were never available to swimmers prior to the 1980s.

13. **Team support at international events.** Team support has evolved into a full staff of massage therapists, physical therapists, sports psychologists, trainers, doctors, chiropractors, and physiologists—much more than Weissmuller would have had accompany him.

14. **Pool technology.** Lane lines, pool depth, and gutters are now thoughtfully designed to reduce surface resistance from waves.

15. **Swimsuit technology.** Suits have evolved from baggy cotton or wool trunks, to nylon, to lycra, to materials that simulate shark skin. In addition, full bodysuits were introduced in the 1990s when it was discovered that an athlete's skin and muscle ripple when fluid forces act upon it, and thus a full-body, tight-fitting suit would keep surface resistance of human tissue to a minimum.

16. **Marketing and sponsorships allowing athletes to compete for more years.** The paradigms on age and performance have taken a dramatic turn, in large part due to sports agents, marketing, and sponsorship dollars that afford swimmers the opportunity to remain in a sport much longer than was the case in Weissmuller's day.

17. **Larger talent pool.** As a result of the Internet, the talent pool around the world now has access to the most current swimming theories, techniques, and training methods.

18. **Pool chemicals.** Salt water provides more buoyancy than tap water, so a pool with salt would positively impact swimming times. I have done no study to determine which chemicals are used at international swimming competitions, or even if there are guidelines to regulate this. Using salt water in pools would be a logical and simple thing to do to improve swimming performance.

19. **Performance-enhancing drugs.** This is an unfortunate truth.

20. **Psychology to meet new standards.** As new world records are set, the bar is raised, and athletes will always look to raise the bar again. There is a psychological component to believing that new standards are possible once a mark is set and that there is a carrot to chase.

If Johnny Weissmuller had been able to take advantage of the 20 items listed here (except the performance-enhancing drugs), then with his high-elbow pull and intuitive feel for the water, I am willing to bet he could have challenged today's world record.

Those of us competing today have benefited from, or have access to, most of what is on the list. We train long hours in the pool to develop aerobic capacities and endurance capabilities, do strength work, eat healthy foods, hydrate, buy expensive swimsuits, streamline, shave down, perfect our starts and turns, and so on, but not one of those efforts will put us in a position to challenge the elite ranks who are tearing up the pool if we do not first have the pull.

I wish you a wonderful new experience in swimming as you embark on discovering the third dimension that lies below you in the water. Enjoy your newfound propulsive power.

FOR BEGINNERS

UNDERSTANDING SWIMMING LINGO
& WORKOUT DESIGN

For those of you who are new to swimming, this appendix is a quick review of some common terms as well as an explanation of how swim-team workouts are designed. After reading this appendix, you will be able to jump in with any team and understand the flow of practice.

SWIMMING POOLS

Any swimming pool that is recognized for competitive purposes is either measured in yards or meters, and if thinking in international terms, then meters is really the only pertinent measurement. The United States is the one country that hosts competitions in a "yard" pool.

Short Course Versus Long Course

Pools come in three different sizes in the competitive swimming world:

- Short course yards: This is a 25-yard pool.
- Short course meters: This is a 25-meter pool.
- Long course meters: This is a 50-meter pool.

There is no such thing as a 50-yard pool, at least not one that is recognized in the competitive swimming community.

"Short course" refers to a shorter pool, one that is 25 yards or meters in length. "Long course" implies a longer pool, hence the distance of 50 associated with it.

If you look at swim-meet results, the front page will nearly always indicate in which length the meet was contested. The abbreviations are as follows:

- Short course yards: SCY
- Short course meters: SCM
- Long course meters: LCM

Distinguishing whether an event was in a 25-yard pool or a 25-meter pool is necessary because a meter is approximately 10 percent longer than a yard. A 100-m freestyle will be approximately 10 percent more distance to cover than a 100-yard freestyle. While the need for distinction between yards and meters is fairly obvious, the part that confuses some people is why swimmers would need to distinguish between a 100-m freestyle held in a 50-meter pool (LCM) versus a 100-m freestyle held in a 25-meter pool (SCM), since the distance covered is the same.

The reason the distinction must be made is due to the flip turns. In a 25-meter pool there are three turns for the 100-m freestyle; whereas, in a 50-meter pool there is only one turn. Since a swimmer generates a great amount of power off the solid wall, the times in a 25-meter pool are faster than in a 50-meter pool.

A Few Further Notes on Swimming-Pool Lengths

1. The Olympics is always contested as LCM—in a 50-meter pool.

2. Most high school and collegiate competitions in the United States are contested SCY—in a 25-yard pool.

3. The international organizing body for swimming, Fédération Internationale de Natation (FINA), began to recognize SCM world records—those set in a 25-meter pool—in the early 1990s. Before then, only LCM world records were recognized.

4. If you are on vacation or traveling for business, you will want to check the length of the pool you are using. You may wonder why you are going slower if you unknowingly find yourself in a 25-meter pool when you normally train in a 25-yard pool.

WORKOUTS: HOW THEY ARE DESIGNED

Workouts in swimming generally follow the same format, no matter which team you join. The workout as a whole is divided into a number of "sets." A set is simply a number of repeats either on a send-off interval or on a rest interval.

Send-Off Interval

This is the most common way to design a set in swimming. Let's use an example: If a coach tells the team that the next set is going to be 10 × 100 on the 2:00, that means the swimmers leave at the 2-minute mark to start the next 100. Some swimmers may finish their 100 in 1:15, so they will get 45 seconds of rest before leaving on the 2:00 send-off. Other swimmers may finish their 100 in 1:40; therefore, they will get 20 seconds of rest before the next 100. This obviously does not seem fair that the faster swimmers get more rest, so that is why swim teams divide swimmers into lanes based on speed. The faster swimmers will have tougher send-off times.

Swimming is a great sport in this sense; there is always a lane for you no matter what your speed. As you get faster, you move up to faster lanes.

Rest Interval

Another way to design a set is to give the swimmers a certain amount of rest after each repeat. The coach may say to do 10 × 100 with 30 seconds of rest after each one. This means that, even within one lane, swimmers may be leaving at different times.

SWIM WORKOUT LINGO

Descending

A coach may say to do 10 × 100 on 2:00, descending 1–5 and 6–10. The "descending 1–5 and 6–10" means that team members are to swim slightly faster on each 100 from number 1 to number 5 and then slow down again on number 6 so that the time is similar to the first 100 of the first 5, but then get faster each of the 100s from 6 to 10.

Times in a descending set may look as follows:

#1	1:30 (the swimmer will get 30 seconds of rest before leaving on the 2:00)
#2	1:27 (the swimmer will get 33 seconds of rest before leaving on the 2:00)
#3	1:25
#4	1:21
#5	1:18 (this is the fastest of the first five; the swimmer gets 42 seconds rest before leaving on the 2:00)
#6	1:30 (this is intended to be easy, like #1)
#7	1:28
#8	1:24
#9	1:22
#10	1:17 (this is the fastest of the second 5)

Building

If a coach says to do 10 × 100 on the 2:00, building each one, then that means to get faster as the 100 progresses. In other words, the first 25 within each 100 would be easy, and then the second 25 faster, the third 25 even faster, and the final 25 of the 100 the fastest. You build your speed as the 100 progresses.

This is different from descending, because in descending there is no change-up of speed within the 100; the change of speed only takes place from one 100 to the next. In building, all 10 of the 100-m (yard) repeats will be similar in overall time (for instance, the swimmer may swim around a 1:26 on each 100), but the coach should see a marked difference in the speed between the first 25 and the last 25 of each.

Negative Splitting

Negative splitting means that the second half of a repeat should be faster than the first half. Going to our example, if a coach says to do 10 × 100 on the 2:00, negative split, then this is similar to building in the sense that the times on each 100 of the set will usually be around the same (as opposed to descending), but negative splitting is different from building in that there is a crisp, clear change of speed at the halfway point of the repeat.

In a negative-split swim, the swimmer will have one speed for the first 50 and then change immediately to the faster speed for the second 50. Building is a gradual change of speed throughout the 100, whereas, negative splitting is an abrupt change at the halfway point.

AN EXAMPLE OF A WORKOUT

The following is an example of how a workout might look if written out on a chalk-board at the pool, or as some coaches do, printed on paper and handed to the swimmers in each lane. This is presented so new swimmers have an idea of how a variety of training options can be put together to form a full swim session.

Warm-up 800 choice. This means you can do any stroke you want, or kick, pull, or whatever, for an 800, no interval.

4 × 150 @ 2:50 (first 50 drill, second 50 kick with no board, third 50 build freestyle). From the previous discussion, you know that 2:50 is your send-off interval, and you know what "build" means for that last 50 of each repeat.

20 × 25 @ 0:50 all out, your choice of stroke

8 × 100 free, swim, descend 1–4 and 5–8 @ 2:00

10 × 50 kick, your choice of stroke, negative split (make the second 25 faster than the first 25), 0:20 rest after each 50

Warm-down 200 easy

TOTAL DISTANCE: 3,400

TOTAL TIME: approximately 1¼ to 1½ hours

That's it. All of the sets between the warm-up and warm-down are intended to train various energy systems, strokes, and techniques. If you know about send-offs, rest intervals, descending, building, and negative splitting, then you can hang with any team in the world. Nuances of individual coaching styles can be picked up easily.

ASK AN OLYMPIAN
ANSWERS TO COMMON QUESTIONS

1. Is it better to breathe on alternate sides or breathe to just one side?

Many coaches will tell you that it is important to breathe on alternate sides in order to develop a balanced, even stroke. The truth is that it does not matter. There are many top swimmers who breathe on alternate sides and also many who breathe every stroke on one side. As an individual, you have your own unique internal rhythm as well as comfort level for how much oxygen you need. If you breathe to one side only and your distance per stroke is not affected, nor your rate of turnover, then you have no worries.

I prefer alternate breathing. It happens to be the perfect rhythm for me and gives the right amount of oxygen. But breathing patterns are not the vital element to the swim stroke.

If you choose to incorporate alternate breathing into your stroke, then be aware that it will feel awkward for the first few weeks. After those few weeks, however, it will begin to feel quite natural and rhythmic. Also, be aware that your normal breathing side will always feel better than the other side.

2. How important is kicking? Should I do a six-beat kick or a two-beat kick?

Again, you are a unique individual, so your kick should match the rhythm of your stroke. Some of the top swimmers have a two-beat kick and others have a six-beat kick.

The swimmers who have a two-beat kick tend to have shorter strokes. They get less distance per stroke but have much quicker turnovers. The two-beat kick provides little or no propulsion. In fact, the swimmer primarily needs only ensure that the kick does not get in the way of the speed generated by the arm stroke.

A swimmer with a six-beat kick will tend toward a longer extension reach of their stroke out front (*not* a glide). The six-beat kick aids the arm and shoulder strength requirements necessary to get into the high-elbow position from such an extended position. The kick, in other words, provides a supportive propulsion during this strenuous portion of the catch.

While a six-beat kick is not a prerequisite to swimming fast, there is a trend in the elite swimming world toward a six-beat kick, and I believe that is due to the relatively recent emphasis on strength training in the top programs. The advances made in strength training lend a shoulder strength that is nicely supported by, and that nicely supports, a six-beat kick. The benefits of this are that swimmers with a six-beat kick have more options for stroke-rate adjustments during a race. Those swimmers may base their race strategies around a slower tempo during the first half of a race and a quicker tempo during the last half (or the last 50).

Take the men's 200-m freestyle in Beijing, for example: Peter Vanderkaay, bronze medalist, swam the first 100 meters of the 200 at a tempo near 1.6 seconds per full stroke cycle. On the third 50, he quickened his tempo approximately one-tenth of a second faster per cycle, and on the last 50 meters, he quickened his tempo another one-tenth second to approximately 1.4 seconds per cycle. This was not a haphazard situation; it was a well-thought-out race strategy.

Triathletes in a longer open-water swim should not be concerned with changing tempo during a race. Settling into a consistent stroke rate for the entire swim is ideal unless there is a strategy to separate from the pack at some point.

You may be wondering how you should kick. If you have a two-beat kick, then it is not important to know how to kick. The goal is to keep the legs balanced, in rhythm with the arm cycle, and out of the way. The technique of kicking is much more important for six-beat kickers.

Ankle flexibility is a big indicator of whether or not you will have a strong kick. Just as our forearm and hand hold the water, so our foot and lower leg should too. The theories of propulsion that we discussed earlier apply just as much to kicking as they do to pulling. Feel the resistive forces against your foot and lower leg. Hold the water as you apply a propulsive force to it. Ankle flexibility is required in order to hold the water in this manner.

The only way to get ahold of the water in freestyle kicking is to have the knee slightly bent on the down-kick. Look at the photo in Figure B.1. The leg applying force to the water is bent. If the knee is not bent, then the leg is like a wooden board pushing up and down against the water. This gives zero forward propulsion. Next time you go to a pool and kick, think about the hold on the water, with a supple, pliable foot and leg, applying force in a direction that moves you forward. The strength will come from your hip flexor and upper leg, but it is the foot and lower leg that hold the water.

After finishing the down-kick, keeping the leg straight on the up-kick is extremely important, unless you are one of the rare people who are able to hyperextend the

FIGURE B.1

A STRONG FREESTYLE KICK REQUIRES ANKLE FLEXIBILITY, A BENT LEG DOWN-KICK, AND A STRAIGHT LEG UP-KICK.

knees. Assuming you are not one of those people, if you bend the leg on the up-kick, then you are applying pressure to the water in the opposite direction of what you just did on the down-kick.

Although next to impossible to believe, a fair number of triathletes and swimmers actually move backward when they kick because of a bent-knee up-kick. The answer for this frustrated crew is to simply focus on not bending the knee on the up-kick. A straight-leg up-kick will, at minimum, keep them from going backward, and if they go one step further and concentrate on holding the water with the foot and leg on the down-kick, they might enjoy forward propulsive kicking for the very first time in their lives. This is always cause for great celebration!

3. Is the use of fins in training good or bad?
I have several answers to this question:

- For beginners: bad
- For swimmers who want to feel fast without feeling the water and doing the work: bad
- For swimmers who are looking for a power- or strength-training workout: good

Using fins as a crutch is the worst thing a swimmer can do, and I see them used in this manner frequently. New swimmers who should be learning to feel the water will oftentimes put on fins (or be told to put them on by a coach who does not understand the importance of holding the water with one's own limbs to generate propulsive forces) as a way to gain confidence. This slows the learning process, because every moment you are using fins means that you have lost that moment for developing true feel.

There are many wonderful drills and exercises that beginners can do to develop the true feel for the water, as were shared in Chapter 6. Please apply those and enjoy the journey that makes you an authentic swimmer.

The other group of people who are equally guilty of using fins as a crutch are swimmers and triathletes who are 100 percent product oriented. They are primarily

FIGURE B.2

FIN TRAINING IS IDEAL FOR BUILDING POWER INTO YOUR KICK BUT SHOULD NOT BE USED BY NEW OR INEXPERIENCED SWIMMERS AS A CRUTCH FOR FEELING THE WATER.

concerned at practice with winning or, at minimum, keeping up with the people in their lane. They want to go fast at the races but have no long-term view for crafting an amazingly propulsive stroke that will help them accomplish this.

Only two groups of people should be training with fins:

1. **People who swim for exercise and recreation.** If the use of fins brings this group more enjoyment, then wonderful. They were never concerned with speed in the first place. They know their purpose, and they have called the suit.

2. **Swimmers and triathletes who intend to purposefully build a specific training effect.** Competitive swimmers and triathletes who understand the high-elbow and have developed a feel for the water with both their arms and legs know that the use of fins can be valuable for building strength, endurance, and power. They do not use the fins for a false sense of security. They use them for a specific training effect. (See Figure B.2.)

Note, however, that in one particular situation it is appropriate for new swimmers, or anyone for that matter, to use fins in order to "keep up" with other people during training. If you attend an open-water swim training session with a group of people who are faster than you, and if the fins allow you to keep up with the group, then you should definitely use them. No person should swim in the open water alone.

4. How much hip roll is too much or too little?

Just as the S-pull pattern has been taken to extremes by some swimmers (see Chapter 5), so too has the idea of rolling the hips. This misinterpretation is like the "telephone game" we all played as children: one person whispers in the ear of the person sitting next to them a short message, and the message then gets spread around the room in whispers until the last person states it out loud to the group. The numerous translations usually distort the message drastically.

Passing on advice about swimming technique is no different from the telephone game. People everywhere, with very good intentions, repeat what they have heard from someone else about technique, but along the way vital information is left out or misinterpreted.

Hip roll is one of the components of technique that anyone can parrot to another person. In fact there is an entire scenario that plays out regularly each day around the world. It goes like this:

You are a new swimmer, and you go to the pool with a friend who has been swimming for awhile. He or she very kindly watches your stroke and gives you a few pointers. You swim two lengths of the pool, and because you have never really swum before and have never read a word about swim technique, you swim fairly flat—not much core engagement or hip roll.

Your friend standing on the deck says to you, "You need to roll your hips." You have no idea how much to roll your hips. Your friend, who is just repeating what someone once told him or her, has no idea either. You figure more must be better, so you rotate so much that you almost tip over onto your back each time.

Now, if I were there and so bold as to interrupt this scenario, I may not have the energy to explain about propulsion, high elbows, and feel, but at least I would stop you from overrotating your hips. I would explain the following:

If a swimmer overrotates the hips, then every other part of the body must wait for the hips to finish. We need to remember that swimming is a synchronous sport; no component of the stroke can move at a rate faster than the others. The pull should determine your rate of turnover; therefore, every other aspect to your stroke should match the rhythm of that.

Hip rolling in and of itself does not propel us forward. Try it. Get in the water with your arms either at your sides or out in front of you and, without applying force upon the water with your limbs, rotate your hips all you want. You will not move forward.

The most important function of the hip roll is to accentuate the power from the propulsive pull. Use the hips enough to maximize your power, but remember that additional hip rolling beyond that not only gives zero return but is actually detrimental to the overall rate-of-turnover side of our important equation (Number of Strokes) × (Rate of Turnover) = Time.

You do not even know what propulsion or rate of turnover means, so you stare at me blankly. I just ruined your day, because you were feeling pretty good about yourself for having done so beautifully what your friend told you to do. I walk away thinking, I need to write a book.

5. Why not pull with a straight arm?

You may wonder why there has to be a bend in the elbow to have an effective underwater pull. You may ask, if the goal is to hold the water, then doesn't it make more sense to hold it with the entire arm as one long lever rather than only the forearm as a much shorter lever? Good instinct. There has indeed been a revolution in this direction—but only in the world of sprinting!

The straight-arm freestyle requires a massive amount of stability, power, and strength that must be developed specifically in training. Sprinters who are attempting to develop this strength must be able to handle the extra resistive force that they get by holding more water, and the strength required can only be sustained for a short amount of time (the 50 freestyle and in a few instances the 100 freestyle). (See Figure B.3.)

Keep in mind that a straighter arm is a longer arm, so it takes a longer path through the water. Anyone who attempts to apply more resistive force with the longer lever should check that their turnover rate is not negatively affected. The key to achieving a fast turnover with the longer lever is to have an extremely powerful core drive. Swimmers who choose to go this route should understand every implication as well as commit to an intense functional strength-training program that includes a strong base of shoulder and core stability and strengthening exercises.

The straight-arm freestyle technique is not discussed in this book because I am assuming that most readers are either triathletes (competing in longer distances than the 50 or 100) or masters swimmers who are over 40 years old, like I am, and who, like I, just pray that something doesn't snap. For age-group swimmers (and some masters swimmers) who are sprinters, discuss with your coach whether or not you should work on a straight-arm pull.

FIGURE B.3

MARGARET SWIMMING WITH THE STRAIGHT ARM TECHNIQUE THAT SHE USES IN THE 50 AND 100 FREESTYLE

DRILL VIDEOS

The videos linked with these QR codes show a variety of drills that develop a strong underwater pull and feel for the water. To access, download a barcode/QR code scanner application (many free options are available online) on your smartphone or computer with optical capabilities. Open the application and scan the barcode. You will be sent a video that shows the techniques described in this book. If you do not have scanning capabilities on your phone or computer, then please visit www.swimspeedsecrets.com/video to view the videos or to find additional drills that are posted there.

While viewing the videos, be sure to watch them both in real time and in slow motion. Real time helps you to see the flow and dynamic energy of the drill, and slow motion enhances your understanding of the finer details of the movements. Review the information in chapters 5 and 6 as you watch. The information in those chapters will remind you of the ingredients in a great pull as well as how to do each one of these drills. When you go to the pool to practice these, do not rush through them; the focus and intended purpose is technique rather than speed.

STREAMLINE DRILL

HALO BENCH
& TUBING DRILLS

PRESS-OUT DRILL

SCULLING DRILL

OUT-OF-WATER
DRILL

CATCH-UP DRILL

ONE-ARM DRILL

ONE-ARM PULL
WITH KICKBOARD

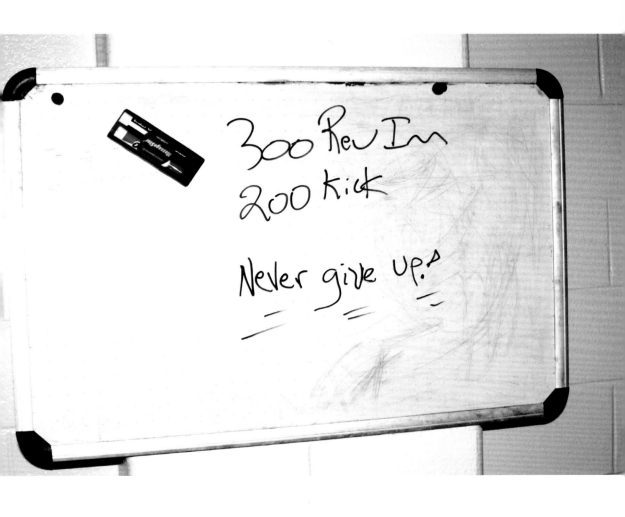

REFERENCES

Colwin, Cecil. 2002. *Breakthrough Swimming. Champaign*, IL: Human Kinetics.

Colwin, Cecil. 1999. *Swimming Dynamics*. Chicago: Masters Press.

Colwin, Cecil. 1992. *Swimming into the 21st Century*. Champaign, IL: Leisure Press.

Counsilman, James. 1994. *The New Science of Swimming*. Englewood Cliffs, NJ: Prentice-Hall.

Counsilman, James. 1968. *The Science of Swimming*. Englewood Cliffs, NJ: Prentice-Hall.

Crawford, Matthew B. 2009. *Shop Class as Soulcraft*. New York: Penguin Books.

Maglischo, Ernie. 2003. *Swimming Fastest*. Champaign, IL: Human Kinetics.

Maglischo, Ernie. 1982. *Swimming Faster*. Palo Alto, CA: Mayfield Publishing.

Weissmuller, Johnny. 1930. *Swimming the American Crawl*. London: Putnam.

INDEX

ABOUT THE AUTHOR

At just over 5 foot 2 inches tall, and not having made her first Olympic team until the age of 27, Sheila Taormina seems an unlikely candidate to have competed in four consecutive summer olympiads in three completely different sports (swimming, 1996; triathlon, 2000 and 2004; and pentathlon, 2008). Her first two attempts to qualify for the Olympics in swimming (1988 and 1992)—during what were considered her "peak" years—came up short. Following those years, she moved forward with her education, finished her master's degree in business in 1994, and then began a professional career in the automotive industry, working a full-time salaried position in Detroit.

With her eyes set on the possibilities of 1996, she trained before and after work with her small, hometown swim team in Livonia, Michigan. There were no corporate endorsements fueling the effort—just a plan, some hard work, and a coach who believed along with her. Sheila learned about technique, efficiency, and the keys to success. Applying those throughout the years, Sheila grew to become Olympic champion in one sport, world champion in a second sport, and the World Cup standings leader in a third sport.

In the end, Sheila Taormina experienced six different disciplines on the Olympic stage—swimming, cycling, running, pistol shooting, fencing, and equestrian show jumping. Her perspective on the Olympics, human potential, and performance is unparalleled.

Today Sheila travels extensively, from San Francisco to Bangkok to Johannesburg and everywhere in between, teaching the swim techniques from her book. She is also a popular corporate keynote speaker, relating the productivity and performance tools she used as an Olympic athlete to those of business executives across the globe.

Visit www.sheilat.com for more information.

STEAM COMING OFF POOL IN EARLY MORNING AT MARINE CORPS BASE, CAMP PENDLETON, CALIFORNIA

CREDITS

Cover design by *the*BookDesigners

Cover and interior photos by Daniel Smith, except for p. 30 by Brad Kaminski, pp. 56 and 118 by iStockphoto, and p. 151 by Stan Gerbig

Mike Troy and Mark Spitz photos (pp. 47, 53, 61, 68, and 122) permission to reprint from Indiana University, The Counsilman Center for the Science of Swimming

Johnny Weissmuller (p. 3) photos permission to reprint from International Swimming Hall of Fame

Illustrations by Nicole Kaufman

The Halo Swim Training System™ is a trademark of Lane Gainer Company

Interior design and composition by Vicki Hopewell

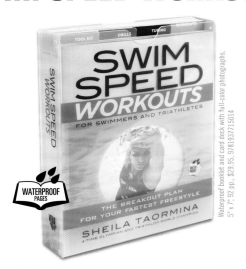